780

AS Music
Revision Guide

OCR

Huw Ellis-Williams

R• RHINEGOLD
EDUCATION

3 SEP 2012

www.rhinegoldeducat

Also available from Rhinegold Education
GCSE, AS and A2 Music Study Guides (AQA, Edexcel and OCR)
GCSE, AS and A2 Music Listening Tests (AQA, Edexcel and OCR)
AS/A2 Music Technology Study Guide, Listening Tests and Revision Guide (Edexcel)
Revision Guides for GCSE (AQA, Edexcel and OCR), AS and A2 Music (Edexcel, AQA and OCR)
Key Stage 3 Listening Tests: Book 1 and Book 2
AS and A2 Music Harmony Workbooks
GCSE and AS Music Composition and Music Literacy Workbooks
In Focus guides: Romanticism, Baroque Music, Musicals, and Film Music
Music Technology from Scratch
Understanding Popular Music

First published 2012 in Great Britain by
Rhinegold Education
14–15 Berners Street
London W1T 3LJ

www.musicroom.com

© Rhinegold Education 2012
a division of Music Sales Limited

You should always check the current requirements of the examination, as these may change. Copies of the OCR specification can be downloaded from the OCR website at www.ocr.org.uk or may be purchased from OCR Publications, PO Box 5050, Annersley, Nottingham, NG15 0DL. Telephone: 0870 870 6622   Email: publications@ocr.org.uk

OCR AS Music Revision Guide
Order No. RHG206
ISBN: 978-1-78038-243-2

Exclusive Distributors:
Music Sales Ltd
Distribution Centre, Newmarket Road
Bury St Edmunds, Suffolk IP33 3YB, UK

Printed in the EU

10071796

Contents

The author

Huw Ellis-Williams was brought up in Bangor and studied in Oxford and Exeter. A pianist, organist and part-time composer, he teaches at a comprehensive school in north Wales where he is head of sixth form, and he is also an examiner for OCR. Huw has a particular interest in instrumental music of the early 20th century, and in music for theatre and film. He is author of the Rhinegold OCR AS Study Guide and co-author of the Rhinegold OCR A2 Study Guide, and has contributed to *Classroom Music*.

Acknowledgements

The publishers would like to thank Richard Knight for his contribution to this publication.

Introduction and About the Exam

In order to gain your AS in Music with OCR, you will need to complete the following sections:

- G351 Performing Music 1 – assessed by a visiting examiner, worth 40% of total AS marks
- G352 Composing 1 – assessed by your teacher, worth 30% of total AS marks
- G353 Introduction to Historical Study in Music – a written exam marked by OCR, worth 30% of total AS marks.

The focus of this revision guide will primarily be on the written examination, Unit G353. In particular, you will find:

- Material to help you prepare for the aural extracts in Section A
- Guidance on revising your prescribed works for the short answer questions in Section B
- Checklists to encourage thorough knowledge of the contexts of your prescribed works for Section C
- Advice on how to write good essays that will enable the examiners to award high marks in Section C.

Also in this book you will find advice on making final preparations for your performance recital, including the *viva voce* discussion, and there is also a section with recommendations for how to approach and complete your composition work.

Remember: your final result not only reflects how musical, intelligent and enthusiastic you are; a large factor is how well you have done what the examiners want you to do. There are no marks available for the fantastic performance you gave in the Christmas Concert or how many books you have read about your prescribed works, how many hours of listening to music you have put in over the past six months or the hours you have spent preparing for a big gig with your band. The examiners can only give marks for how well you have done the tasks required of you in the OCR specification, and they can only do this according to their published mark schemes. This book is intended to help you access as many of those marks as your other skills allow, and not trip up over the business of taking the exam.

Good luck!

Top ten tips

1. PLAN YOUR USE OF TIME

AS Music comprises many different challenges. You will also have other subjects to think about at this very intense time. If too much gets left to the last moment, none of it will get the focus required to do well. Therefore think in advance about which unit you are going to focus on and when, and benefit from the feeling that everything is under your control.

2. CHOOSE THE PROGRAMME FOR YOUR RECITAL WISELY

You may be working towards a high grade examination on your instrument, but if the difficulty of the music makes you tense and nervous, this will not be the right music for your AS performing. Make sure the music you choose for your recital is within your technical ability and comprises pieces that you enjoy playing.

3. MAKE SURE YOU HAVE THOUGHT ABOUT THE MUSIC YOU ARE PERFORMING

Your discussion with the examiner about your pieces is worth 20 marks, and good preparation can secure a high mark however well the performance goes. Furthermore, thinking through answers to likely questions about your chosen pieces and the way you play them well in advance is likely to improve your performances.

4. MAKE SURE YOUR EXERCISES FOR SECTION A OF THE COMPOSING UNIT MEET ALL THE REQUIREMENTS

There have to be seven exercises in all; two need to have fully written out inner parts; one needs to be in a minor key. Overlooking these requirements will cost you marks, without doing anything wrong musically.

5. MAKE SURE THAT YOUR COMPOSITION OR ARRANGEMENT SHOWS THAT YOU HAVE TAKEN CARE

You may have been very successful in your compositional work, but you need to communicate this through a well presented score and a well performed and produced recording, or else the success of your work can be easily obscured to the moderator.

6. TRAIN YOUR EAR REGULARLY

In Section A of Unit G353, you will have to respond to music that you have not studied, but this does not mean that you cannot prepare. The relevant parts of your body (ears and brain) need training. A sprinter would spend many weeks getting into shape before an important race; you need to be listening to, and thinking about, music from the repertoire that you are going to respond to in the exam over a long period of time before you sit the exam. Remember that listening is not the same as hearing. Having music on in the background whilst you are thinking about something else is hearing; listening means you are concentrating solely on the sounds reaching your ears. This is what you need to do in the exam. Make sure you are in training.

7. USE YOUR INSTRUMENTAL SKILLS TO PLAY YOUR PRESCRIBED WORKS

Whatever instrument you play, you can engage with the music you are studying practically. If you are very fortunate you will belong to an orchestra or jazz band that can read through some of the pieces during a rehearsal; but even if this experience is not available to you, you can play or sing some part of the music somehow. The combination of reading the notation with the concentration required to play the music whilst hearing the resulting sounds is a tremendous boost to your brain, which has to cope with the challenge of assimilating all the information about the music.

8. IF YOU ARE STUDYING THE PRESCRIBED ORCHESTRAL WORKS, READ YOUR SCORES IN SILENCE, JUST LIKE A BOOK

As you sit reading this revision guide it is not necessary for you to be reading it aloud: the words make sense to your eyes, and, if you like, you can imagine the sound of someone saying the words out loud as you read. The same should be true for your reading of a musical score. If you have listened to the music often enough (and not just heard it!), you should be able to read the score and imagine the sound inside your head. This is a huge advantage when it comes to answering questions in the exam room. So let your eyes follow the scores at the tempo of the music and enjoy your own personal performance inside your mind!

9. REVISE METHODICALLY

You have three different pieces to prepare with various angles to each. Structure your revision so that each session focuses on one work from one particular angle. Jumping from one piece to another with no clear sense of what angle you're looking at will not help you consolidate your knowledge and understanding.

10. PRACTISE WRITING ESSAYS FOR SECTION C

Writing an essay about a piece of music is a specific skill: do not leave it to the exam room to try it for the first time, however well you have revised. Make sure that you support the points you make with specific examples from the music, and that you make good use of musical vocabulary. Your essay needs to be well structured too.

Unit G351 Performing Music 1

About the unit

The Performing unit is in three sections:

Section A (60 marks)	
Recital	
What you do: Perform as a soloist on an instrument or voice, no longer than 8 minutes in total.	*You must:* ■ Submit copies of your music (chord patterns or lead sheets if improvised) to the examiner before the day of the examination. The examiner will contact your centre for these. ■ Arrange an accompanist if you need one.

Section B (20 marks)	
Discussion (*viva voce*)	
What you do: Answer questions from the examiner about your recital. The discussion will last about 5 minutes. You may illustrate what you say on your instrument or voice.	*Aspects to be covered:* ■ Decisions in preparing and performing your pieces: expressive (tempo, phrasing, dynamics, colour) and technical (bowing, breathing, fingering, pedalling, amplification). ■ A discussion of how these decisions were realised in your performance.

Section C (40 marks)	
Extended performing	
What you do: Choose one of the options for further performing.	Option 1 *Performing on a second instrument or voice:* ■ The instrument or voice must have a clearly different technique or repertoire from Section A. ■ No longer than 4 minutes.
	Option 2 *Performing in an ensemble or a duet, or as an accompanist:* ■ No longer than 4 minutes.
	Option 3 *Performing your own composition(s):* ■ One or two pieces written for your instrument/voice (as in Section A) and one or more different instruments. ■ No longer than 4 minutes. ■ Hand your fully notated score to the examiner.
	Option 4 *An improvisation (no longer than 2 minutes, with 10 minutes preparation), using one stimulus provided by OCR:* ■ Four pitches (without rhythm) ■ A melodic incipit (beginning), available in different clefs; may be transposed if needed ■ A rhythmic incipit ■ A simple poem (with optional melodic incipit) ■ A chord sequence (with keyboard accompaniment).

The examiner will record all sections of the exam. You may have an audience present (if you wish) for your performances in Section A and in Options 1, 2 and 3 in Section C.

Section A: The recital

You will be examined between February and May by a visiting examiner from OCR. This may happen at your school or college, but you might be asked to travel to another local centre. If that is the case, it would be a good idea to check it out: how large is the room? What is the acoustic like? What are the warm-up facilities? And (for pianists) what is the piano like?

Half the marks for this unit (60/120 – that's 20% of your total AS marks) are for the Section A Recital. As you prepare for the 'big day', consider the following four areas that the examiner will be assessing. Each receives a mark out of 15.

KNOWLEDGE AND FLUENCY

How correct is your performance? In particular:

- Does your performance have the correct notes?
- Is your playing rhythmic, without hesitations or slowing the tempo for the difficult bits?
- Is your sense of knowing what comes next so instinctive that the result is a truly fluent performance?

TECHNICAL CONTROL

How confident and assured is your approach to your instrument? This will depend on your instrument. For example:

- **Piano**: Are your hands well co-ordinated? Do you have a good range of touch on the keyboard with secure fingering? Do you have good control of the pedalling?
- **Strings**: Do you play with precise intonation? Do you produce a rich tone with good bow control and a natural vibrato? Are technicalities such as pizzicato, harmonics and double-stoppings confidently handled?
- **Woodwind and brass**: Is there a good tone across the full range of your instrument? Do you have secure breath control? Is there clear articulation through good tonguing that co-ordinates with fingering?
- **Percussion**: Do you have good stick control? Are rolls played evenly? Is the use of foot pedals precise? Are effects such as rim shots and playing on the bell of the cymbal successful? Are ringing sounds dampened at the correct moment?
- **Singing**: Is your intonation secure? Is diction clear? Is there a good tone quality that is even across the range of the voice? Is breath control reliable?

REALISATION OF PERFORMANCE MARKINGS AND/OR CONVENTIONS

There is more to performing than just playing the right notes. Usually there is much more in the score, and sometimes there are aspects to the style of the music which need to be part of a performance. For example:

- Is your performance at the correct tempo?
- Have you followed dynamic markings and the composer's indications for phrasing and articulation?

- Have you included ornamentation in the correct way, either as indicated or in keeping with the style of the piece?
- Have you used alterations to the printed rhythm in idiomatic fashion, such as rubato in Romantic music and swing patterns in jazz?

AURAL AND STYLISTIC UNDERSTANDING

Is there a sense that you have stepped outside your own focus on the challenges of being the performer to consider the overall effect on your audience (which includes the examiner…)? In particular:

- Are you projecting the character of the music to your audience, or merely concentrating on producing the correct notes?
- Is there an overall sense of style that suits the music?
- Can you be seen, or are you hiding behind the music?
- Is the balance with your accompanist successful? This may include sections where you need to play softer for a melody in the piano to be heard.
- Has the use of amplification been appropriately controlled?

The examiner will take care to match the criteria for marking your particular recital to the instrument and repertoire that you are presenting.

Examiners also take into account the level of difficulty of the pieces that you are playing. The specification suggests that pieces of about Grades IV and V are suitable for higher marks. Grades III and IV would be suitable for medium-band marks. When you are choosing your pieces you should pick something which suits your level of difficulty. Bear in mind that it is better to perform something you can play well and play musically than to struggle through something difficult. If you have to keep slowing down to play the tricky passages, perhaps you should consider another piece. Make allowance for nerves on the day as well. Be sure to discuss your choices with your teacher.

PREPARING FOR YOUR RECITAL

Top quality performances are the end result of a long process of preparation. If you get this process right, the recital becomes something you look forward to: you know you are ready, and you want to share your music-making with other people, even the examiner! You can get a big buzz from the performance, in a way that is probably not possible from other AS exams. This mood transfers itself to your playing and to the atmosphere in the venue and is bound to secure a high mark from the examiner.

On the other hand, insufficient preparation, or leaving too much to the final week before your recital, is likely to increase your tension and make you more nervous. This makes it much harder to project your musical instincts in the recital and is likely to make your listeners nervous too. The examiner will be more aware of any shortcomings in your performance and the mark is likely to be a good deal lower overall.

So, well before your recital date you should:

- Choose your recital programme, making sure that the pieces are well within your abilities.
- Select contrasting pieces that show different skills and sides to your musicianship.

- Establish a regular practise schedule, and make sure that any difficult passages receive plenty of slow practice.
- Organise an accompanist (if you require one) well in advance and have several sessions together so that you can share ideas and support each other in the pressures of performing music together.
- Try recording yourself playing so you can listen with 100% focus on how your performance is sounding and think of ways to improve it.
- Arrange a run-through of your recital in the room where the exam will be so that everything is familiar come the day of the recital.

On the day itself you should:

- Aim for a good night's sleep beforehand.
- Arrive in good time for the exam.
- Tune and warm up before you go into the room, and check your tuning again before you start.
- Sometimes reading your music through without playing can be a beneficial tactic: imagine the performance you are about to give inside your mind.
- Enjoy performing the music that you have spent a lot of time preparing, and if you are feeling nervous, take some deep breaths and stay calm.

Section B: The discussion (*viva voce*)

After your recital performance, you will have a short discussion with the examiner about the music you have just played and how you went about performing it. This is sometimes called the *viva voce*.

This is worth a further 20 marks towards the performing unit, so it is best not to leave it to chance. The main focus of this discussion is the way you played the pieces in your recital. This may involve:

- Decisions you made in preparing your performance regarding tempo, dynamics, articulation and tone colours: were these dictated by the score, a recording, or your own ideas about the music?
- Your thoughts on the emotional content of the music and how you tried to communicate this to your audience: how does the music create this aspect, and how did you highlight it in your performance?
- Any issues that arise from realising the intended expressive content from the instrument you play: what thought has to be given to issues such as bowing, breathing, pedalling, variety of tone quality, etc. in order to enhance your performance?
- The extent to which you succeeded in your expressive intentions in the performance that you have just given: were you listening to your own performance and aware of what went well and anything that might have been a little better?

TOP TIPS FOR THE DISCUSSION

1. Preparation

The discussion about your recital is only 5 minutes long. Five minutes is a long time if you have no idea what to say, but you also need to use the time wisely to give the examiner the best information and impression of you, so don't leave it to chance. You'll be more relaxed if you plan, so think about what you might want to discuss in advance.

Try making a list of things to discuss: how you perform, technical and expressive aspects, the decisions you made when you practised. Jot your ideas down on a piece of paper or draw a diagram to pin up on your bedroom wall. Add new ideas to it as you think of them.

2. Practising

Just as you practise your instrument, practise talking about your own performance. Discuss your pieces with your teacher or another musician, and as you do so, check that you know the vocabulary of performing – tempo, articulation, dynamics, phrasing, colour. Which technical words (bowing, fingering, chest voice, embouchure, breathing, pedal, and so on) belong to your instrument or the voice?

What would you change or try to do better next time? Acknowledge difficulties and challenges, and be specific about aspects of your performance you want to improve or a particular passage that needed more practice.

It is helpful to look at the markings in the score. How are you responding to them? Which marking did you think about most when you practised? Are there detailed markings in the score? Do you have to add details of expression to your performance?

3. On the day

The examiner will choose what they want you to discuss, probably starting with a topic that they think will get you off to a good start. They may then choose a specific passage or phrase to talk about, or you may get a chance to choose. Be confident about using your instrument or voice to demonstrate some of the points you discuss. Don't let modesty stop you talking about what went well – you should be able to talk about aspects of your performance that went as you planned. Most of all, try to enjoy talking about your performance and show the examiner that you think about what you do. The examiner is trying to find out what kind of musician you are, and the chances are you play because you enjoy it, so stay relaxed and let your passion for your performance come through.

Section C: Extended performing

The remaining part of your Performing unit is called Extended Performing and is worth the last 40 marks of the 120 marks available for this unit. For this section you choose one task from a list of four:

■ Performing on a second instrument or voice
■ Performing in an ensemble
■ Performing your own composition
■ An improvisation.

If you are choosing one of the top two on this list, the task is very similar to your main recital, and all the advice given earlier in this chapter regarding good preparation and the criteria for assessment will be relevant to you here.

If you prefer to perform your own composition, much of the advice given earlier in this chapter about your recital is also relevant. In addition, as the composer of the music that is going to be performed, you need to think carefully about the following aspects:

- Are you sure that all the musical demands of your piece lie well within the capabilities of your players and their instruments?
- Have you made good use of the capabilities of the instruments that you have chosen for your piece, and their potential for creating some interesting textures and variety of timbre?
- Have you prepared easy-to-read parts for all the musicians who are going to play your piece? You may need to deal with transposing instruments. Rehearsal cues, such as 'Figure A', are also useful.
- Have you indicated in the music your ideas about changes of dynamic, articulation and tempo, so that your intended expressive content is apparent to the performers and, in turn, to the audience?

If you prefer to take the Improvisation option for Section C, you will be able to choose **one** from **five** different stimuli that the examiner has as a basis for your improvisation. These are:

- Four pitches
- A short melodic phrase
- An unpitched rhythm pattern
- A short poem, with optional melody for the opening line
- A chord sequence.

Once the examiner has given you your chosen stimulus, you will have 10 minutes to prepare your improvisation before you then play it for the assessment. In this time you should:

- Think logically
- Try to construct methodically an overall shape to your improvisation
- Remember how your piece starts, and (if possible) the way you intend to end, as you cannot write anything down.

Some of the marks are for your use of the stimulus, so you might like to practise your improvising with these thoughts in mind:

- **Four pitches**: What melodic shapes can they make through various orders and octave displacements? Do they make an interesting (if dissonant) chord? Could you use them for a bass riff? Can you use them as four long pedal notes one after another?
- **Short melodic phrase**: Does it work well in sequence, up and down? Can you break it into two halves? Is there an effective and easy to remember upside-down version (the inversion)? Does it change into the minor key well?
- **Rhythm pattern**: Can you build up the intensity well by increasing the dynamic and the texture? Does it break naturally into two halves, each of which can be repeated for a while before the other appears? Does it work well at a variety of tempos?
- **Poem**: Does the structure of the poem suggest a melodic line that can return in various places (as a refrain or the opening to each verse)? Are there good moments in the poem for dynamic contrasts, particularly high or low notes, or intense silences?
- **Chord sequence**: Is there a variety of texture or figuration with which you can play the chord sequence? Does the pattern suggest any melodic ideas to you? Might the middle section of your improvisation be in a different key, either transposing the chords or changing between major and minor?

Unit G352 Composing 1

About the unit

Composing is a coursework unit. Your centre has to complete its assessment of your work (and that of others in your class) and submit marks to OCR by 15 May. Your centre should let you know the final date by which they require you to finish and submit your work.

The unit is in two sections:

Section A (45 marks)	
The Language of Western Tonal Harmony	
What you do: A set of seven exercises (in major and minor keys): ■ Six completed during the course ■ One exercise under centre supervision near the end of the course.	Each exercise consists of a melody, chosen by your centre, 8–24 bars in length. *You must:* ■ Add a bass line ■ Indicate harmonies, using roman numerals, guitar chords or figured bass ■ Complete at least two exercises in full texture in the style of a given incipit (beginning).
Section B (45 marks)	
Instrumental Techniques	
What you do: Choose one option:	Option 1 *A composition for between four and ten instruments:* ■ No longer than 3 minutes ■ May include acoustic and/or amplified instruments ■ Full score and recording required.
	Option 2 *An arrangement of a lead sheet for between four and ten instruments:* ■ No longer than 3 minutes ■ May include acoustic and/or amplified instruments ■ Full score and recording required ■ Written commentary on the process of composition, including relevant listening required ■ The original lead sheet to be submitted.

Section A: Exercises

Marks are awarded under three headings:

HARMONIC LANGUAGE (20 MARKS)

To write successful harmony, you first have to know what key the music is in. Remember that the key signature will fit both a major and a minor key, so double check for further evidence before deciding. The last note is often the tonic; also a minor key will use an accidental to sharpen in the 7th degree in many places.

Once you know your key, work out the available chords. Chords I, IV and V could be enough in most cases, but II (especially), III and VI add welcome variety and show that you can use a range of chords.

Knowing which chord goes well requires you to sense which are the most significant notes in the melody and choose chords that are consonant with these. Every note offers three possibilities, because it could be the root, 3rd or 5th of the chord at that point.

Chords usually change on the downbeat of each bar, but look out for opportunities for additional changes elsewhere to bring variety to the harmonic rhythm (the rate of chord changes).

Careful consideration should be given to the end of each melodic phrase. What cadence is implied? The chances are that the chord at the end of each phrase should either be the tonic (for perfect and plagal cadences) or the dominant (for imperfect cadences) with the possible surprise of chord VI for an interrupted cadence.

TECHNIQUE (15 MARKS)

Good technique concerns how you use the notes of the chords you have chosen between the various parts of the texture and whether this results in a good musically aware solution to the exercise.

In particular, you should give careful consideration to the bass part: does it have a good flow, with plenty of conjunct motion that is easy to sing, but with some strong leaps of 4ths and 5ths at the cadential points? Using 1st inversion chords can often help to iron out an awkward bass line.

You also need to consider the relationship of the melodic line to the bass. It is important that they do not move together in parallel octaves or 5ths. A good effect is having the main notes in the melody a 3rd or 6th above the bass (probably in a higher octave too) and 1st inversion chords can help in this regard too.

In the exercises you submit that have a complete texture (which two examples in your portfolio need to have) the examiners will also be looking for good technique in the way you have continued the opening texture. Ask yourself whether you have been consistent in continuing the pattern in the texture as given at the start.

NOTATION (10 MARKS)

It is very important to submit your exercises in a way that communicates precisely and legibly the notes that you intend to be examined. Any illegibility or ambiguity will count against you.

Score-writing software is usually the preferred method to ensure clarity; if this is your choice, make sure that you understand all the issues relevant to the tasks you are needing it to do for you. If you prefer to use pencil and manuscript paper, always be mindful of setting out your score clearly, using a ruler for barlines and taking care over the proper vertical alignment of simultaneous events in the rhythm.

Make sure you label your chords clearly and correctly. Roman numerals are probably best, with capitals for major chords and lower case for minor ones (in a major key this makes for I, ii, iii, IV, V and vi), but guitar-style chords are acceptable with inversions shown using the slash chord convention (e.g. Dm/F).

Section B: Instrumental techniques

For this section you have a choice of two tasks:

- Write an original composition for between four and ten instruments
- Make an arrangement of a lead sheet for between four and ten instruments.

In either case, the resulting piece must be no longer than 3 minutes. The submission should include a full score and a recording. For the arrangement the original lead sheet should also be included.

Marks are awarded under four headings:

MATERIALS (10 MARKS)

In this area credit will be given for the quality of the main ideas that you have used in your composition, or – in the case of the arrangement – the extra ingredients that you have introduced to the music beyond what is found on the lead sheet. This will involve four potential aspects:

- Melodic material (including countermelodies)
- Bass material (including, where appropriate, riffs and ground bass phrases)
- Rhythmic material
- Harmonic material.

USE OF MEDIUM (15 MARKS)

Credit will be given for writing idiomatically for the instruments that you have chosen to use in your composition, and exploring their expressive capabilities. It may be a good idea to write for an instrument that you have long experience of playing; alternatively you might write for an instrument that is played by a good friend. Whichever instruments you choose, however, be mindful throughout the composing process of the following issues:

- **Practicality**: are you writing something that is playable? This goes beyond the compass of the instrument. Remember that wind players need to breathe, pianists' hands have a limited stretch, and not all double-stopping on a string instrument is possible.
- **Range**: how do each of your chosen instruments sound in the extremes of their ranges? The violin is very rich in its lowest register, while the oboe becomes rather thin in its upper register. Use these aspects creatively, and do not get drawn into putting every note on the stave. Remember the ledger line, and even the octave sign or changes of clef!
- **Dynamic**: some instruments are associated with being loud (e.g. trumpet) but all offer a range of tone colour and expressive capability depending on the dynamic requested. For example, a soft high clarinet can be very serene, whereas a loud high clarinet has considerable force and is able to pierce. Be aware of some difficulties: the oboe finds playing its lowest notes softly very difficult, for example.
- **Special effects**: many instruments offer a distinct change of tone quality through special playing techniques. Strings can play pizzicato, brass instruments can use mutes, some instruments (including the harp) can play harmonics, singers can hum. Using such techniques can not only broaden the expressive range of your piece, but help with the sense of structure too.

TECHNIQUE (10 MARKS)

Good compositional technique is the process through which the chosen material for a piece is developed and combined together to make an effective and interesting overall structure.

There are an almost limitless number of specific techniques that can lead to a successful piece and no one piece is going to use more than a small number. However, the composer who is not prepared to think about technique through the composing process and in relation to all music elements is highly likely to produce an unsuccessful composition that is too random and ultimately loses the interest of the listener.

Much comes down to balancing the two more important principles of composition: repetition and contrast. If a musical idea is a good one, it is worth repeating it. This underlines it in the listener's mind as being significant. The repetition, however, is an opportunity for some contrast, maybe of register, dynamic or instrumentation. Later on, greater contrast will be needed, maybe of rhythm or melodic shape. More significant still would be a change of key or metre; this might introduce the middle section of the piece.

COMMUNICATION (10 MARKS)

The best composers in the world have to be able to communicate their musical ideas to others, both the performers and the listeners.

For your AS submission it is very important that the score is accurate and well presented. Make sure that it contains not only the notes of your piece, but all the performance directions too, such as tempo, dynamics and phrasing. Don't overlook to indicate which instruments you are writing for too. Your best bet might be to use some good score-writing software, but it is fine to submit a hand-written score: just make sure it is clearly legible!

You also need to submit a recording of your piece. Both the performance and the recording quality need to be good, so do not leave either aspect to the last minute. If you need assistance with this, make sure you ask for help early on.

Unit G353 Introduction to Historical Study in Music

About the unit

Unit G353 Introduction to Historical Study in Music is sometimes known as the 'listening exam'.

You will be given:

- A question paper. You will write your answers in this.
- An insert to the question paper, which contains copies of the notated music that you need. You will answer some questions on this insert, so don't forget to hand it in at the end of the exam.
- A CD, with a spoken introduction to the exam and the extracts of music on which the questions are based.

Other points to remember:

- You should also have a personal stereo with headphones, which you will use to play the music. Your school or college will advise you about this. If you have to supply your own, make sure that you can skip forward and backwards and that it has a time display in minutes and seconds. This will help you locate passages of music quickly if you want to listen to them without having to replay the whole extract. If your CD player is not powered by the mains, make sure that you fit it with new batteries on the day of the exam.
- Your examination centre should supply you with manuscript paper (lined music paper for writing out music examples in notation).
- You can ask for extra writing paper if you need it.

The exam starts with 15 minutes preparation. During this time you should:

- Listen to the music on the CD and familiarise yourself with the order of the excerpts
- Read the question paper
- Consider in particular any questions where you are required to compare two different excerpts
- Perhaps choose which question you will answer in Section C.

You are not allowed to write during this time.

Including the preparation time, the exam is 2 hours in length, which gives you 1 hour 45 minutes to write your answers.

There are three sections to the paper:

Section A (30 marks)		
Aural extract		
On the CD:	*In the insert:*	*What you do:*
Two extracts of music that you have not studied. ■ **Extract 1A** taken from instrumental music 1700–1830 ■ **Extract 1B** from popular music 1900 to the present day.	A skeleton score of both Extract 1A and Extract 1B.	Answer the questions on one extract only: either Extract 1A or Extract 1B. Do not answer on both extracts – you will run out of time on Sections B and C.
Section B (40 marks)		
Prescribed works		
On the CD:	*In the insert:*	*What you do:*
Extract 2. Two different recorded performances of a passage from **one** of the orchestral works from the 18th century and early 19th century.	A full score of the passage in the recorded extract.	Answer all the questions. *Extract 2 is worth 25 marks.*
*The prescribed orchestral works for **June 2012 to January 2014** are:* ■ Vivaldi: Concerto in E for Bassoon and Orchestra RV 484, first movement ■ Haydn: Symphony No. 103 in E♭ Hob. I:103 ('Drum roll'), fourth movement ■ Beethoven: Concerto in D for Violin and Orchestra Op. 61, first movement.		
On the CD:	*In the insert:*	*What you do:*
Extract 3. A passage from **one** of the jazz recordings you have studied.	There is no score for the jazz recording.	Answer all the questions. *Extract 3 is worth 15 marks.*
*The prescribed jazz recordings for **June 2011–January 2013** are:* ■ Louis Armstrong and His Hot Seven: *Alligator Crawl* (1927) ■ Charlie Parker: *Ko-Ko* (1945) ■ Gil Evans/Miles Davis: *It Ain't Necessarily So* from *Porgy & Bess* (1958). *The prescribed jazz recordings for **June 2013–January 2015** are:* ■ Louis Armstrong and His Hot Five: *Hotter Than That* (1927) ■ Duke Ellington: *Ko-Ko* (1940) ■ Miles Davis: *Boplicity* from *Birth of the Cool* (1949)		
Section C (20 marks)		
Contextual study		
There is no recording or score for Section C.		*What you do:* Write an essay on the historical background to one or more of the prescribed works. There are three questions to choose from. Answer one question only.

Top tips for the examination:

- If you use your own personal stereo, buy new batteries.
- Make sure your pen works. Use a pencil (and rubber) for dictation.
- Choose **either** Extract 1A or Extract 1B – not both.
- Read the questions carefully and follow the instructions.
- Space is limited so control your writing. Ask for extra paper and/or manuscript paper if you need it. Write essays in complete sentences and paragraphs.
- Revise all six of the prescribed orchestral works and jazz recordings. Don't gamble on your favourites coming up, or on last year's choice not being used again.
- Refer to evidence from the music. Use bar numbers.
- There are marks for the insert so be sure to write your name on it and hand it in.

PRACTICE QUESTIONS

Past papers will give you a clear idea of what to expect. These are available on the OCR website, and your centre may have copies of the CDs. The mark scheme is also available on the website.

The following pages of this book will help you to revise for each section of this unit. Make the most of the resources available to you so that you are prepared and know what to expect in your actual exam.

NOTE

Practice questions for Section A (both Extracts 1A and 1B) and Section B (Extract 2 and Extract 3) are published in *OCR AS Music Listening Tests* by Veronica Jamset and Huw Ellis-Williams, published by Rhinegold Education, 3rd edition (2011). There is a CD of the music for each question and the answers are provided for you to check. The latest edition includes useful practice questions for the prescribed orchestral works by Vivaldi, Haydn and Beethoven and the prescribed jazz recordings for June 2011–January 2013 and June 2013–January 2015.

Section A: Aural extract

ABOUT THE UNIT

EXTRACT 1A: INSTRUMENTAL MUSIC 1700–1830

Extract 1A will be two or three short passages from an instrumental piece from the period 1700–1830. Possible composers include Vivaldi, J.S. Bach, Handel, Haydn, Mozart, Beethoven, Schubert or any other composer of that time. A 'variation'-style piece is common, in which you hear a theme and a varied version of it. Alternatively, you may hear the opening theme of a movement (for example in rondo form) and then different treatments of the theme from later in the piece.

EXTRACT 1B: POPULAR MUSIC FROM 1900 TO THE PRESENT DAY

Extract 1B will be in a similar format: two or three short passages of popular instrumental music from 1900 to the present day. A film or TV theme is sometimes used, also instrumental arrangements of songs or extended versions of a theme. Again the passages will feature a theme and one or more varied treatments of it.

CHECKLIST FOR REVISION

You should be aware of the following terms and be able to recognise them in the music. Practise listening to pieces from the period and ticking off the terms as you hear them. Are there any you don't know? You can look them up in the glossary in this book or in your study guide, or ask your teacher. It is not enough to simply be able to recite the word – you need to be able to hear it in the music.

- Acciaccatura, appoggiatura, grace notes, glissando
- Arpeggio, broken chord, scale, ascending, descending, chromatic
- Binary form, ternary form, phrase, anacrusis
- Diatonic, non-diatonic, chromatic, chromaticism
- Imitation, antiphony, call-and-response, countermelody
- Intervals, major, minor, augmented, diminished, octave, 9th, 10th
- Key signatures, major keys, minor keys
- Modulation, dominant, subdominant, relative minor, relative major
- Monophonic, homophonic, polyphonic, contrapuntal, imitative
- Ostinato, riff, dominant pedal, tonic pedal, sequence
- Passing notes, auxiliary notes, appoggiatura
- Perfect cadence, imperfect cadence, plagal cadence, interrupted cadence
- Pizzicato, double-stopping, strumming
- Quavers, semiquavers, demisemiquavers
- Staccato, legato, detached, sustained
- Time signatures, simple time, compound time
- Trill, turn, mordent, tremolo
- Triplets, dotted rhythm, syncopated, augmentation, diminution.

You will also need to be able to identify instruments. Some are easy to recognise – violin, trumpet, piano, bassoon, flute, timpani, but check that you are also able to distinguish between the following:

- Viola, cello, double bass
- Bass guitar, banjo, guitar, harp, harpsichord
- Piccolo, oboe, cor anglais, clarinet, bass clarinet
- French horn, trombone, tuba
- Glockenspiel, xylophone
- Bass drum, snare drum, tenor drum
- Hi-hat, suspended cymbal, ride cymbal.

Which of these instruments can be muted? How does a mute alter the sound?

STRUCTURE

You may be asked to describe the structure of a passage. This is a little like spotting the phrases, sentences, paragraphs and chapters in a passage of writing. In music this means understanding where melodic phrases begin and end (look and listen out for the cadences!) and working out whether the second phrase is an answering phrase to the first (or, at least, a continuation of the same musical thought as the first) or is providing a new idea.

Take time to read the question carefully, and look for how many marks are available as this will indicate how much detail is required.

Top tips:

■ Questions on structure can be answered either using letter names (A, B, C, etc.) or descriptions, or – usually safest – a combination of both.
■ The most basic structures are binary form (AB) and ternary form (ABA). Other shapes are found: ABAB, ABB, AABA and so on.
■ Varied treatments of the same material can be 'letter + number', e.g. AA^1BA^2.
■ Take care with repeat marks and repeats which are written out. AABB can be written as AB, but if the A section has a repeat marked but the B section repeat is varied, written out in full it must be $AABB^1$.
■ Apply letter names to sections in a consistent way. If the section is eight bars long and made up of two identical phrases you can label it either A or AA, but don't call a similar phrase structure something else later.
■ Describe it in words to make it clear – for example, 'Both A and B sections are repeated', 'The first four bars are repeated but changed to end on a perfect cadence'.
■ Comment on phrase lengths ('two-bar phrases', 'four-bar phrases').
■ Refer to the anacrusis (upbeat) if it is a regular feature of the melody.
■ Introductions and codas (outros) are always important. The intro is never labelled 'A': the 'A' section is always the melody.
■ Avoid discussing instruments, dynamics, rhythm, articulation. These are nothing to do with structure.

ANSWERING A QUESTION ABOUT STRUCTURE

The grid opposite shows how examiners might mark a question about structure. The example is for a question with a maximum of 3 marks awarded. To achieve full marks examiners might expect awareness of the general shape (2 marks) and one further point (1 mark). Therefore, the correct answer could look like this:

AA^1BA^2 (3 marks)

or

AABA (2 marks) and one further detail (1 mark).

As further detail the examiner would accept either (i) four-bar phrases, (ii) anacrusis or (iii) change to A phrases.

Look at the sample answers in the grid opposite and how the marks have been allocated.

Sample answers	Examiner's comment	Mark awarded
Candidate A: AABA.	Correct shape, but no further detail.	2 marks
Candidate B: The melody is in four-bar phrases. The first melody is repeated, then a new melody and a repeat of the first phrase.	No letters but an accurate description of shape (first melody = A, new melody = B). Observes that the melody is in four-bar phrases.	3 marks
Candidate C: The melody begins with an upbeat every time. There is a binary form (AB) and a coda which is a repeat of the first section.	Binary is incorrect. Candidate recognises the repeat of the opening material at the end, but this is too confused to gain a mark for shape. Upbeat = anacrusis, so 1 mark.	1 mark
Candidate D: AABA structure. A ends with an imperfect cadence but the second and third A sections have different endings.	Correct shape. The detail of the imperfect cadence for A and then changes for A^1 and A^2 are enough for a further mark.	3 marks

MELODIC DICTATION

There will be one or more questions which require you to complete the notation of a few bars of the score that have been left blank. The rhythm of the missing phrase will be printed over the score, and you have to work out the correct pitches. Often there are two questions, one on a section of melody which will be in the treble clef, and one on a part of the bass which will be in the bass clef.

You are required to write your answer on the score in the insert, not in the question paper. Don't forget to hand this in – the examiner will be looking for it.

Top tips for melodic dictation:

- Before the exam revise the sound of different diatonic intervals (the intervals in a major or minor scale): major 2nd, major/minor 3rd, perfect 4th and 5th, major and minor 6th and 7th, octave. You are marked for recognising the correct intervals in the melody.
- Before the exam, practise recognising chromatic notes and working out what they are. Chromatic notes usually 'stand out' in a diatonic melody. For example, add D♭ or F♯ to a C major scale – note the difference the chromatic notes make.
- Practise humming or singing from notation as much as you can. Believe that melodic dictation is something that you can get better at over time.
- Use a pencil. Have a rubber handy for corrections.
- Listen to the bars you need several times. Get the tune 'in your head' so that you can hear it without having to play the recording.
- The rhythm of the missing notes is printed above the stave. Use the same rhythm in your answer. Watch out for tied notes (e.g. a single pitch written as two tied notes), if there are any.
- You may find that the blank passage you are asked to fill in is very similar to another point in the musical excerpt for which the notation is provided on the score given. Listen carefully, comparing the two phrases: if you can hear that some notes are the same in both locations, you will have found some of the answer already printed for you!

- Are you able to 'test' notes against given notes in the score, such as the first note, the next note or a note in the bass part?
- Does your melody fit the chords and harmony of the music you can hear? Which are the harmony notes?
- When you have completed the notation check it one more time against the recording. Don't leave any gaps – there is 1 mark for the correct shape of a complete melody.

SAMPLE QUESTION

This sample question gives you a guide to the style of the questions and how they are marked. It is based on a well-known melody, which is printed next to the question. In the exam you can listen to the passage several times, replaying the bars as many times as you need. You would write your answer in the correct place on the score, which will be in the insert.

The passage is taken from the opening bars of the first movement of *Eine kleine Nachtmusik* by Mozart.

On the score complete the melody played by the 1st violins in bar 1 to bar 4. The rhythm of the passage is given above the stave.

The number of marks awarded to a fully correct answer varies according to the length and difficulty of the passage. For a question worth 5 marks, examiners might use a mark grid of this type:

5 marks	Entirely correct.
4 marks	One or two errors of pitch.
3 marks	Three or four errors of relative pitch.
2 marks	Five or six errors of relative pitch.
1 mark	The general melodic shape is correct, but with mostly inaccurate intervals between the notes.
0 marks	No melodic accuracy.

Here is some advice from the examiner on how you should approach this question, and on the next page are two sample answers with the marks that would have been awarded.

Examiner's advice

If you find a recording of this famous piece and try to fill in the missing bars on the previous page, you might notice the following things in (approximately) this order:

- The first note which is given (G) is heard again on the strong 3rd beat of the first bar and the downbeat of bar 2 (the 2nd and 4th missing notes according to the given rhythm above the stave).

- The same G is also heard on the weaker 2nd beat of bar 2.
- The note between each of these Gs is the same note each time. By singing it (out loud, if necessary, or silently inside you head) you should be able to count down the scale from the G and find that it is a 4th lower: in other words the D below.
- You now have a good clue to the fact that bar 2 is an arpeggio of G major, and you can confirm this by realising that the last note is the high D – an octave above the recurring lower D.
- You should be able to hear that bar 3 starts one note lower than bar 2 ends – i.e. on the high C.
- You might also realise that the last missing note in bar 4 is our friend the low D that you hear three times in the opening phrase.
- The remainder of the second phrase is somewhat more challenging. You could use your knowledge of the Classical period style to realise that the most likely harmony after 2 bars of the tonic at the start of a piece is the dominant 7th. Careful listening will confirm that this is the case here.

SAMPLE ANSWER 1

Examiner's comments

- Bars 1–3 of the melody are completely accurate.
- There are two errors of pitch in bar 4, marked 'X'. Adjacent notes are correct, so count as two errors.

4 marks awarded

SAMPLE ANSWER 2

Examiner's comments

- The melody begins accurately.
- There are five incorrect pitches in bars 2–3. Some intervals are correct even though the pitches are wrong. There are four errors of intervals, underlined and marked 'X'.
- The G in bar 4 is incorrect. Count as one error because it is between two correct notes.
- Total of five errors.

2 marks awarded

WRITING DOWN A BASS

There is usually a question in which you have to complete a passage in bass clef. The question is similar in style to the melody question, and many of the earlier 'top tips' apply to this question. Many people find the bass question more difficult, usually because the bass is not so easy to hear and follow compared to the melody. If you regularly play or sing from treble clef you may have to work to get your bass clef reading up to the right level.

Top tips for notating a bass line:

- As with melodic dictation, work out a strategy to build up your skills. Matching the notes and the sound you hear is a skill that you can improve.
- Before the exam get to know the bass clef as well as you can. For example, pick out notated bass lines on a piano, hum the bass part of the Drum Roll Symphony along to the CD, or scat sing the bassoon solos from the Vivaldi concerto.
- Revise the diatonic and chromatic intervals in low registers and in bass clef. Leaps of 4ths and 5ths are common in bass lines.
- Bass lines are not melodies. Your work on the bass lines in the exercises for G352 Composing 1 will help you get to know how bass lines behave.
- Do you still have your pencil and rubber?
- Make sure that you are picking out the bass line, usually the lowest notes – cellos, basses, bassoons, bass guitars, piano left hand and tubas are the sounds to follow. Listen to the bass several times to get it 'in your head'.
- As with the melody, the rhythm of the missing notes is printed above the stave and you need one bass note for each of the notes of the rhythm. Watch out for tied notes (e.g. a single pitch written as two tied notes), if there are any.
- Are you able to 'test' notes against given notes in the score, such as the first note, the next note or a note in the melody part?
- Does your bass fit the melody? Does your version of the bass do what you would expect a bass to do? The melody notes may help you identify the chords in the music. Look out for arpeggios or leaps that outline the notes of chords – these are extra clues.
- When you have completed the notation check it one more time against the recording. Don't leave any gaps – there is 1 mark for the correct shape of a complete bass line.

SAMPLE QUESTION

This sample question gives you a guide to the style of the questions and how they are marked. In an exam you would be able to listen to this passage several times. You would write your answer in the correct place on the score, which will be in the insert.

The passage is taken from the opening bars of the second movement of Haydn's String Quartet in C Op. 76 No. 3, known as the 'Emperor' Quartet.

On the score complete the bass played by the cello in bar 1 to bar 4. The rhythm of the passage is given above the stave.

SAMPLE ANSWERS BY THREE CANDIDATES

Look at the answers given by Candidate A, Candidate B and Candidate C. At first glance they look similar. The general shape of the melody and the intervals between the notes are not very different. All three candidates heard the chromatic movement in the bass at the very end of the extract and have tried to include this in their answer, with different results.

Listen to the music. Which do you think is the correct answer?

How many marks did Candidates A and C score? Use the mark grid to help you.

4 marks	Entirely correct.
3 marks	One or two errors of relative pitch.
2 marks	Three or four errors of relative pitch.
1 mark	The general melodic shape is correct, but with mostly inaccurate intervals between the notes.
0 marks	No melodic accuracy.

Examiner's comments

- Candidate A made three errors:
    - The first note should be a minor 2nd (not a minor 3rd) lower from the given G
    - The interval between notes 3 and 4 should be a 5th (not a 4th)
    - The first note of the second phrase should be a 5th higher than the previous note (not a 4th).
  2 marks awarded
- Candidate B is completely correct.
  4 marks awarded
- Candidate C made five errors – although most intervals are inaccurate, the general melodic shape is correct.
  1 mark awarded

WRITING ABOUT THE MUSIC

One or more of the questions for Extract 1A and Extract 1B will ask you to write about the music. The question will usually ask you to 'Describe...', 'Explain...' or 'Compare...', although other instructions can also be found (Identify..., Comment..., How?, Why? and so on). There will be space on the question paper for you to write more than a few words; perhaps two or three sentences or more.

Questions like this might be asked about a number of musical topics, and you will need to be able to use the technical terms and vocabulary relevant to each.

For example, if you were asked to comment on the articulation in a particular passage of music, you would need to be able to recognise (aurally from the recording and visually in the score) legato, marcato, staccato and accents (including sforzandos).

Here are some more sets of important terms:

- **Cadences**: perfect, plagal, imperfect, interrupted
- **Devices**: pedal note, sequence
- **Harmony**: primary triads, secondary triads, major and minor chords, dominant 7th, inversions, circle of 5ths progression, harmonic rhythm
- **Melodic features**: passing note, auxiliary note, appoggiatura, sequence
- **Modulation**: key relationships, subdominant, dominant, relative minor.

Here are some further categories. What relevant terms can you think of for each one? If your mind goes blank, the glossary may jog your memory.

- Ornamentation
- Performing techniques
- Pitch
- Rhythm and metre
- Structure
- Tempo
- Texture
- Tonality.

EXERCISE

1. Make a chart showing the words you might use to answer each of the questions. Use the checklist of words on page 21.

2. Find out the meaning of the words that you are not sure about. If there are too many, break them down into groups to make them easier to learn.

3. Try to relate each topic (and the words that go with them) to your actual listening in both Section A practice and your study of prescribed works for Section B.

There will be more of this type of question in Section B. There are examples of writing about music below in the section about the orchestral works and the jazz recordings. Of course, in Section B you have studied the music, so your answers should be more detailed than in Section A, where you are hearing the music for the first time.

Top tips for writing about music:

■ Read the question carefully. Answer on the exact bars or passage required.
■ Listen to the music and look at the score.
■ Are you being asked to describe, explain or compare?

REMEMBER

'Describe' is looking for an answer based on **what** is happening in the music.

'Explain' is looking for an answer based on **how** something happens in the music or **why** something has a particular significance.

'Compare' is looking for an answer that highlights both the similarities and differences between two passages of music.

■ You may be asked about harmony or tonality, the use of instruments, the treatment of the melody, the accompaniment, or any other aspect of the music. Practise and revise answering different types of questions.
■ Be relevant. If the question asks about tonality, don't start writing about the violins.
■ The number of marks will tell you how much detail is required. Write what you know. The examples below and in Section B are a guide to how marks are awarded.
■ Organise your answer in the order of events in the music.
■ If comparing, describe and explain both: for example, 'Passage 1ii is in compound time but Passage 1i is in simple time.'
■ Use evidence from the music consistently. Don't make too many general points if you can point to specific examples. Use bar numbers to show exactly where. Beat numbers can be written using little numbers: for example, 'the syncopated pizzicato chord at bar 24^4'.
■ Bullet points can be used in Sections A and B. Remember that you need detail and evidence to get the higher grades.

SAMPLE QUESTION

Explain how the instrumentation changes when the melody is repeated at bar 16 to bar 23. (*4 marks*)

For this question the mark scheme indicates the following answers. You gain a mark for each of the points identified in the mark scheme.

■ Melody in violins (1), instead of solo flute (1)
■ Sustained/bowed/arco (1) chords (in strings), previously tremolando (accept tremolo) (1)
■ Pizzicato (1) cellos/double basses/bass (1)
■ Harp added (1).

There are seven possible points for which you can get a mark.

Look at the sample answers to this question on the next page. All the statements are correct but only the relevant and precise ones gain marks.

SAMPLE ANSWER 1

> The melody is in the violins with the harp. The other strings are playing all the way through.

Examiner's comments

- Violins and harp are mentioned
- No credit for strings. The question is about changes at bars 16–23.

2 marks awarded

SAMPLE ANSWER 2

> The flute melody is now played by the violins with strings playing chords arco. The double basses are playing pizzicato notes on the offbeats.

Examiner's comments

- Flute and violins are correct. The candidate clearly understands that the violins have the melody at bars 16–23 and the flute had it originally
- Arco, double basses and pizzicato are mentioned
- Clear and accurate detail, hitting five of the points on the mark scheme.

4 marks awarded

SAMPLE ANSWER 3

> The melody is louder with more instruments playing. The chords are strong and clear. The melody changes from minor to major.

Examiner's comments

- No specific points of instrumentation identified: 'more instruments playing' is too general
- Minor to major is about tonality, so not relevant.

0 marks awarded

Section B: Prescribed works

The three prescribed orchestral works and the three prescribed jazz recordings will take up a significant amount of time in your course. The questions for both Section B and Section C are based on these works. Altogether, questions on the prescribed works account for two-thirds of the marks on the AS paper.

It is important that you get to know these works well over a period of time. Each work should get about the same amount of attention. Only two of the six works will come up in Section B, but the others can feature in the essay questions in Section C. Students who try to guess in advance which works will feature in this year's paper are often disappointed.

Work out a strategy to learn the information you need. You are expected to be familiar with these works so study them in advance and revise regularly. If you rely on your common sense and general musical knowledge to get you through, you will miss out on the detail and technical vocabulary that will get you a good mark.

There are practice questions for these prescribed works in *OCR AS Music Listening Tests* by Veronica Jamset and Huw Ellis-Williams, 3rd edition (Rhinegold Education, 2011) which will enable you to prepare for what to expect and how to handle the questions.

The following section deals with the different types of questions that you can come across. Some of the questions overlap with Section A. You may be asked again to: write about texture, structure, tonality or scoring; comment on composing devices; or identify articulation, chords, melodic devices or performing techniques. An important difference is that this time you are expected to know the work. Your answers will therefore be more detailed and show more depth.

To practise the sample questions in this section you will need to have the scores of the set works to hand. You will most likely have been provided with copies to study by your school or college, but if not you can find them online at http://imslp.org.

Prescribed orchestral works

Top tips for the prescribed orchestral works:

- Learn all three works equally. Don't leave it too late to start revising.
- Listen to more than one recording of each work, including performances on historical instruments ('period performance') or (if there are any) historic recordings.
- Go to a live professional performance if you can. If not, search for one online. Take care to find a good quality orchestra: either one from a major city (the London Symphony Orchestra, for example) or one of the specialist period instrument groups such as the Orchestra of the Age of Enlightenment.
- Get to know the printed score well. The layout may be different when you see an extract in the exam.
- Follow the score when you listen. For variety choose different sections to focus on. Hum along with solo or bass parts.
- If you have a spare score or a photocopy (enlarge to A3 to get the print to a good size), highlight important features. Write comments, symbols or diagrams for your revision.
- Make sure you are familiar with the various notations and terms used in the score and understand the significance of each. Also, check that you understand the implications of any transposing instruments that are involved so that you can answer any transposition questions.
- If the music stops, can you explain what comes next? Can you describe the music that comes before any passage you choose?
- Learn the structure of the work, so that you can locate any passage. Knowing the keys will help you place some sections.
- Learn how to work out chords from a full score. Look at the bass first, then check the notes in violins, flutes and oboes, then against transposing instruments. Does your chord sound as if it might be correct?

SIGNS AND TERMS

You are expected to know the meaning of signs and terms used in the scores. Here is a checklist – do you know them all?

VIVALDI: BASSOON CONCERTO

- Allegro poco – 'A little lively'
- solo – a passage in which the bassoon plays solo (accompanied by basso continuo)
- ⌢ – pause
- tr. – trill
- tutti – a passage in which the whole orchestra plays.

HAYDN: SYMPHONY NO. 103 IN E♭, 'DRUM ROLL'

- a2 – both players on the stave play in unison (e.g. 1st and 2nd oboe)
- Allegro con spirito – 'Lively with spirit'
- cresc. – getting louder
- *ff* – fortissimo (very loud)
- *fz* – forzando (an accent)
- ⌢
- I solo – 1st player only (e.g. 1st horn) has the most important part of the texture
- soli – all players on the stave play in unison and have the most important part of the texture.

BEETHOVEN: VIOLIN CONCERTO

- a2
- Allegro ma non troppo – 'Lively but not too much'
- arco – play with the bow
- cresc.
- dimin. – getting softer
- dolce – gently
- espressivo – expressively
- *ff*
- pizz. – plucked
- poco cresc.
- *pp* – very soft
- sempre *p* – always soft
- sempre *f* – always forte
- sempre *ff*
- *f*
- *sfp* – sforzando-piano (sudden accent and then immediately soft)
- solo
- sul D e G – play all the notes using only the D and G strings
- tr. (in the timpani) – a drum roll on the timpani
- tutti.

Also, check that you are familiar with all the usual ways of notating ornaments, tremolo and divided strings.

TRANSPOSING

There is usually a question about the notation of transposing instruments (clarinets, horns and trumpets) or instruments which use the alto or tenor clefs. You will be given a short passage to write out to show that you understand how it sounds. For example, you may have to write out a part for Horn in E♭ at sounding pitch.

You need to know:

- The alto clef for the viola parts in all three orchestral works
- The tenor clef for the bassoon parts in Haydn and Beethoven.

Examples:

Beethoven: Violin Concerto, bars 270–272, bassoon parts in tenor clef:

You would need to write the passage in the treble clef as follows:

And in bass clef:

In Beethoven's Violin Concerto, bars 37–39, the violas use the alto clef:

Make sure you know how to write this out in another clef, for example in bass clef:

Top tips for the clefs:

- Remember that the alto and tenor clefs are C clefs, showing where middle C goes
- Check that your answer fits with the melody and harmony of the other parts in the score
- Remember also that the double bass is written an octave higher than it sounds.

Transposition (i.e. writing a part in another key) applies only to woodwind and brass instruments. There are no transposing instruments in Vivaldi's Bassoon Concerto. The transposing instruments in the Haydn and Beethoven works are:

Prescribed work	Instrument	How does a written C sound?	Sounding pitch
Haydn: Symphony No.103 in E♭, 'Drum roll', fourth movement	Clarinets in B♭	Clarinet C sounds as B♭	A tone lower than written
	Horns in E♭	Horn C sounds as E♭	Major 6th lower than written
	Trumpets in E♭	Trumpet C sounds as E♭	Minor 3rd higher than written
Beethoven: Violin Concerto in D Op. 61, first movement	Clarinets in A	Clarinet C sounds as A	1½ tones lower than written
	Horns in D	Horn C sounds as D	Minor 7th lower than written
	Trumpets in D	Trumpet C sounds as D	Major 2nd higher than written

EXAMPLES

Here is an example for each of the transpositions used by Haydn and Beethoven. If you understand how to transpose already, you may wish to hide the answers and use them as exercises.

Study these examples. These suggestions may help you:

- Write the key signature in before you start. If you are in the treble clef, use the same key signature as the violins, flutes and oboes (the instruments which never transpose).
- Pencil in the first note of your answer. Use the 'sounding pitch' guide on page 33 to help you. Make sure the first note is correct: does it fit the harmony in the strings, flutes, oboes or bassoons?
- Complete the other notes. Check that the intervals in the melody and the harmony are the same as in the original.
- If you have the correct key signature, only notes with an accidental (sharp, flat or natural) in the original need one in the answer. Look at the examples to see what happens to accidentals.
- Note that accidentals can change (e.g. from flat to natural) when the notes are written at sounding pitch. Check intervals of tones and semitones to make sure you work out the correct accidental.

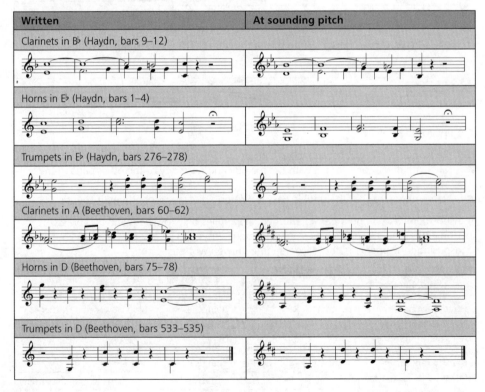

Written	At sounding pitch
Clarinets in B♭ (Haydn, bars 9–12)	
Horns in E♭ (Haydn, bars 1–4)	
Trumpets in E♭ (Haydn, bars 276–278)	
Clarinets in A (Beethoven, bars 60–62)	
Horns in D (Beethoven, bars 75–78)	
Trumpets in D (Beethoven, bars 533–535)	

A brief summary of the structure of each work is given here. Check that you are familiar with the shape of each work.

VIVALDI: CONCERTO IN E MINOR FOR BASSOON AND ORCHESTRA (FIRST MOVEMENT)

Section	Instrumentation	Keys
Ritornello	Full orchestra	E minor
Solo 1	Bassoon and continuo; violins	
Ritornello	Full orchestra	B minor
Solo 2	Bassoon and continuo	
Ritornello	Full orchestra	A minor E minor
Solo 3	Bassoon and continuo; violins	
Ritornello	Full orchestra	E minor

HAYDN: SYMPHONY NO. 103 IN E♭, 'DRUM ROLL' (FOURTH MOVEMENT)

Rondo form	Sonata form	Keys
Theme (A) bars 1–107	Exposition First subject	E♭ major B♭ major
Episode (B) bars 107–157	Second subject	B♭ major (B♭ minor)
Theme (A) bars 158–182	First subject	E♭ major
Episode (C) bars 182–263	Development	C minor (D♭ major, F minor)
Theme (A) bars 264–316	Recapitulation First subject	E♭ major
Episode/Coda (B) bars 316–399	Second subject Coda	E♭ major (E♭ minor)

BEETHOVEN: CONCERTO IN D FOR VIOLIN AND ORCHESTRA (FIRST MOVEMENT)

Ritornello form	Sonata form	Keys
1st ritornello bars 1–88	Tutti Exposition	D major (D minor)
Solo 1 bars 89–223	Solo Exposition	D major A major
2nd ritornello bars 224–283	Development	(F major) A major (A minor) C major
Solo 2 bars 284–364		B minor, then various other keys, most notably G minor
3rd ritornello bars 365–385	Recapitulation	D major (D minor)
Solo 3 bars 386–496		
4th ritornello bars 497–510		
Solo cadenza bar 510		
Coda bars 511–535		D major

VIVALDI: BASSOON CONCERTO IN E MINOR

SAMPLE PASSAGE

Look at the extract from bar 46 to the end of the movement.

Are you able to:

- Explain all the terms and signs used in the passage?
- Write out the viola part in treble or bass clefs?
- Work out the keys and modulations?
- Identify the chords used at any point?
- Explain where the extract comes in the structure of the movement?
- Describe the music that comes before this passage?

QUESTION

Describe the variety of Vivaldi's writing for the solo bassoon in this passage. (6 marks)

There are six marks for this question, so examiners will probably use a marking grid to assess your answer:

6 marks	The answer accurately identifies and describes a wide range of relevant musical details. Supporting evidence is identified precisely.
4–5 marks	The answer accurately identifies and describes a number of relevant musical details. Most supporting evidence is identified generally.
2–3 marks	The answer accurately identifies and describes a few basic relevant musical features. Supporting evidence is limited or partially accurate.
1 mark	The answer makes some relevant and accurate comment on the music, with little or no supporting evidence.
0 marks	The answer makes no relevant or accurate comment on the music.

SAMPLE ANSWER 1

The bassoon solo begins with a melody in repeated pairs of semiquavers, with wide leaps between low and high notes. In bars 50–53 there is a sequence using fast demisemiquaver broken chords. There is an extended passage in triplet semiquavers at bars 54–56, using the high register. The articulation has four slurred notes followed by two detached notes. The solo ends with a descending scale in Scotch snap rhythm (bars 57 and 59).

Examiner's comments

■ The candidate identifies four different types of writing ('semiquavers', 'demisemiquaver broken chords', 'triplets … high register', 'descending scale in Scotch snap rhythm').
■ There is understanding of further specific details in the bassoon writing ('wide leaps', 4 + 2 pattern of articulation).
■ The location of the evidence is clear and exact ('begins', consistent use of bar numbers, 'ends').

6 marks awarded

SAMPLE ANSWER 2

The bassoon writing is difficult. There are long passages in semiquavers and triplets. The bassoon plays a sequence with the violin trills.

Examiner's comments

■ The candidate identifies two different types of writing ('semiquavers', 'triplets') but there is no supporting evidence (e.g. bar numbers). There is understanding that there are 'long passages'.
■ There is no evidence of any detailed understanding. The references to 'sequence' and 'the violin trills' are not relevant – no credit for these.

1 mark awarded

SAMPLE ANSWER 3

Vivaldi uses a wide range in his solo, e.g. range of two octaves in bars 48–49. There are demisemiquaver arpeggios and scales. Triplets are used in semiquavers in bar 55 with articulation.

Examiner's comments

- The candidate identifies three different types of writing ('demisemiquaver arpeggios', 'scales', 'triplets … in semiquavers').
- There is some detailed understanding ('range of two octaves'). The point about 'articulation' is not clear – more explanation needed.
- Some evidence is specific, with correct bar numbers.

4 marks awarded

HAYDN: SYMPHONY NO. 103 IN E♭, 'DRUM ROLL'

SAMPLE PASSAGE

Look at the extract from bar 107 to bar 157.

Are you able to:

- Explain all the terms and signs used in the passage?
- Write out the viola part in treble or bass clefs?
- Work out the keys and modulations?
- Identify the chords used at any point?
- Explain where the extract comes in the structure of the movement?
- Describe the music that comes before this passage?

WRITING ABOUT HARMONY AND TONALITY: SAMPLE QUESTION

Describe features of the harmony and tonality in this extract. (*5 marks*)

SAMPLE ANSWER 1

The passage changes key all the way through. The main tune is passed around the orchestra in different keys, e.g. the cellos and basses, flute. It goes from tonic to dominant and back. Bassoon in tenor clef so notes are flat. The work is in E♭ but this part uses C♭ and finishes on A♭ and D in the violins. The bass holds a B♭ at the end.

EXERCISE

Can you explain why an examiner would give this answer 0 marks? Write down what improvements you would make to this answer to get more marks. The mark grid is similar to the other mark grids you have seen so far. Use it to remind yourself what the examiner is looking for.

4–5 marks	The candidate accurately locates and describes a range of keys and chords, demonstrating knowledge of features of tonality in the work.
2–3 marks	The candidate locates and describes a number of keys and chords with some accuracy. There is limited awareness of features of tonality in the work.
1 mark	The candidate identifies very few keys and chords accurately and/or there is basic awareness of features of tonality in the work.
0 marks	There is no accurate comment on keys and chords.

Now compare your answer with the examiner's comments on this answer.

Examiner's comments on sample answer 1

- The candidate does not describe keys and harmonies accurately. Phrases such as 'changes key' and 'in different keys' are too general, sounding too much like guesswork.
- 'From tonic to dominant and back' shows an attempt to describe tonality, but it is incorrect.
- The reference to E♭ ('the work is in E♭') is not enough to merit a mark. The key of the symphony is given at the head of the section.
- The reference to the held B♭ is not linked to a chord or key. This also applies to other references to pitch in this passage.

Only a small amount of accurate and relevant detail is needed to improve the answer. For example, here is the sample answer again with three significant changes (highlighted). Compare the two answers:

Sample answer 1a

The passage changes key all the way through. The main tune is passed around the orchestra in different keys, e.g. the cellos and basses, and flute **in B♭ major**. It goes from **major to minor** and back. Bassoon in tenor clef so notes are flat. The work is in E♭ but this part uses C♭ and finishes on A♭ and D in the violins. The bass holds a B♭ **pedal** at the end.

Examiner's comments

- The candidate identifies some keys and chords accurately, including the change to the minor key and the return to major.
- The bass B♭ is identified as a 'pedal' and located at the end.
- There continues to be some confusion with the comment about the bassoon. The reference to A♭ and D in the violins does not refer to tonality or harmony. The candidate has done enough for the 2–3 band of marks.

3 marks awarded

Examiners will have a long list of possible correct answers, but you don't have to spot all the possibilities to get full marks. Aim to make a number of accurate points backed up by specific evidence.

SAMPLE ANSWER 3

> The passage begins in the dominant key, B♭ major. The music changes suddenly to B♭ minor at bar 121. It returns to the major key at bar 133 with a sudden B♭ major first-inversion chord, alternating with F⁷d in faster harmonic rhythm. After repeated perfect cadences (bars 140–146) there is a linking passage (to modulate back to the tonic), uses chromatic chords over a dominant pedal note on B♭, bars 147–157. The C in the flute makes a dominant 9th chord (bar 153). The last chord is a dominant 7th chord in the tonic key, E♭ major.

Examiner's comments

- There are a number of accurate and specific references to keys and chords. Bar numbers are used consistently and effectively.
- References to inversion chords, perfect cadences, dominant pedal, chromatic chords and dominant 9th show a clear and detailed grasp of tonal harmony.
- There is easily enough accurate evidence here to award full marks.

5 marks awarded

BEETHOVEN: VIOLIN CONCERTO IN D

SAMPLE PASSAGE

Look at the extract from bar 43 to bar 64.

Are you able to:

- Explain all the terms and signs used in the passage?
- Write out the clarinet, French horn and trumpet parts at sounding pitch?
- Work out the keys and modulations?
- Identify the chords used at any point?
- Explain where the extract comes in the structure of the movement?
- Describe the music that comes before and after this passage?

DESCRIBING TEXTURE: SAMPLE QUESTION

Compare the textures used in the passage at bar 43 to bar 50 and at bar 51 to bar 64. (*6 marks*)

Texture concerns the relationship between simultaneous lines in the music, covering the number of parts, their function and register. The question may not feature the word 'texture', however, a question such as: 'Comment on the nature of the writing for the orchestra in this passage' is asking about a similar concept.

You have to describe what you hear. Don't be tempted to sum the texture up in a single word unless there is only one mark for the question. If there are six marks you are expected to make a series of points and to provide evidence. You have the score to help you identify instruments and see exactly what they are playing.

A starting point is to describe the melody, accompaniment and bass. Explaining what each part does in turn goes a long way towards describing how they work together.

	Bar 43 to bar 50	Bar 51 to bar 64
Melody	Full woodwind section, chordal/homophonic, in thirds, flutes high, clarinets middle, bassoons low.	Violins in octaves. Woodwind section double the melody in thirds at bar 60.
Accompaniment	1st violins repeated A, dominant pedal. Sustained octaves in horns with the bass.	Quaver triplets in violas/cellos in octaves, contrary motion, countermelody. Pedal in horns, trumpet, timpani until bar 56.
Bass	Pizzicato bass notes separated by silences.	Pizzicato bass, faster movement.

Notice words such as chordal, homophonic, thirds, octaves, double, contrary motion, countermelody. These words suggest the idea of instrumental parts working together to create a musical texture. Others include: harmony, polyphonic/contrapuntal, canon, fugal, antiphonal/antiphony. 'Monophonic' is also useful to describe a single sounding pitch (for example the first violins at bars 39–42 or the timpani in the opening bar) or sometimes unaccompanied octaves.

PRACTICE EXERCISE

Try writing an answer to the question on the previous page. Write in sentences and include detailed evidence. Don't look at the grid above after you have started, but you can look at the score.

SAMPLE PASSAGE

Look at the extract from bar 511 to the end.

Are you able to:

■   Explain all the terms and signs used in the passage?
■   Write out the French horn parts at sounding pitch?
■   Work out the keys and modulations?
■   Identify the chords used at any point?
■   Explain where the melodic material for this passage is used elsewhere in the movement?
■   Explain where the extract comes in the structure of the movement?
■   Describe the music that comes before this passage?

COMPARING TWO PERFORMANCES

The sample question below is based on extracts from two different recordings of the Beethoven Violin Concerto:

■   Extract 1: Joshua Bell (violin), Camerata Salzburg, Sir Roger Norrington (conductor). Sony Music, ASIN B0000646Z2. Track 4, 22:31–23:46.
■   Extract 2: Henryk Szeryng (violin), Royal Concertgebouw Orchestra, Bernard Haitink (conductor). Classic FM The Full Works CFM FW 075. Track 1, 24:46–26:06.

SAMPLE QUESTION

Compare the two performances of this music. Comment on the similarities and differences between them. You may wish to refer to aspects such as:

- **The performance of the solo part**
- **The orchestral accompaniment**
- **Tempo**
- **The overall sound of the recording. (8 marks)**

There are eight marks for this question, so examiners would probably use a marking grid like this to assess your answer:

7–8 marks	Specific and consistent evidence of aural perception from a range of musical features from both extracts. Perceptive, well-constructed comparisons.
5–6 marks	Evidence of aural perception from a range of musical features from both extracts. A range of effective comparisons, perhaps lacking some detail.
3–4 marks	Some evidence of aural perception from a range of musical features from both extracts. An attempt to make effective comparison between recordings.
1–2 marks	Limited and/or basic evidence of aural perception, perhaps from one recording with little effective comparison between recordings.
0 marks	The answer makes no relevant observations from either recording.

You should note that the first point that examiners are looking for is evidence of aural perception. This means you have to describe in detail what you hear and explain what it means.

Top tips for comparing performances:

- Listen carefully to both extracts, following the score in the insert. Make quick notes on the important points. Cover the bullet points given in the question and any other points that you notice.
- Are there places in the performance where the performer has changed what the composer has written?
- Circle or mark any evidence in the score, e.g. dynamic or expression marks, which you can write in quickly.
- Similarities may be asked for, but most of your best points will be differences.
- For most comparisons, describe both performances and use the bar number to pinpoint the exact place to listen for the evidence.
- Write in paragraphs, not bullet points and ask for more paper if you need it.
- Don't express a preference; describe what you hear: for example, 'The orchestra in Extract 1 is louder and more rhythmic', not 'The orchestra in Extract 1 is better.'
- Check your answer. Make sure you have not missed anything important. A common mistake is to mix up the two recordings, writing 'Extract 1 is faster' when you meant to say 'Extract 2 is faster'.

In these sample answers all the statements about the performances are correct. The aim of this exercise is to look at how the marks awarded are affected by the amount of evidence that is included. To make this clearer, incorrect descriptions have been left out. You get credit for your correct observations, but usually incorrect statements bring your mark down.

Look at the three sample answers. The mark grid on the previous page will help you to understand how the marks have been awarded.

SAMPLE ANSWER 1

> The solo in Extract 1 is quieter than Extract 2, who uses lots of vibrato. The orchestra is also quieter. There are many changes of tempo in both recordings. The recording balance of Extract 1 makes the orchestra sound far away.

Examiner's comments

- A number of points are made, all of them correct and covering a range of aspects. There is some attempt at comparison, but limited to dynamics ('quieter').
- There is some understanding of the use of vibrato, changes in tempo and recording 'balance' but most comments are not supported by any detail or supporting evidence.

3 marks awarded

SAMPLE ANSWER 2

> The performances are similar because both violinists play quietly in the melody after the cadenza. The solo in Extract 2 plays with vibrato and the notes sound legato and expressive. He uses a slide between B and G (bar 517). The solo in extract 1 is quieter. Both performances start slow and get faster toward the end and finish loudly. The second orchestra is a full symphony orchestra, but Extract 1 has a chamber orchestra. The bassoons are louder in bar 523, not *pp*, in Extract 2.

Examiner's comments

- A range of points are made, mostly in a general way with little supporting evidence or detail.
- There is a good point about the vibrato and expression in Extract 2 with some evidence – the portamento at bar 517. The observation on the bassoon volume is backed up with a specific reference to a point in the score.
- There is some comparison of differences – the quieter solo in Extract 1, the size of the orchestras.

5 marks awarded

SAMPLE ANSWER 3

Extract 1 begins more slowly and quietly than Extract 2. The pizzicato strings are quieter in 1; in Extract 2 there are more strings and you can hear the bass clearly. The soloist in Extract 2 plays with stronger tone and vibrato on the G and D strings; the solo in Extract 1 is piano, with less vibrato.

In Extract 1 the solo is faster for the crotchets at bar 517, and there is an accelerando in the second half of the melody. Extract 2 doesn't get faster until the bassoon solo at bar 523. There is more variety in tempo in Extract 2, e.g. faster at the solo in bars 525–526. The second bassoon phrase is much faster and the final tutti at bar 531 is allegro.

The soloist in Extract 2 uses stronger sforzando accents on beats 1 and 3 in bars 531–533. He changes bow more often than the one bow in a bar that Beethoven wants. The solo in extract 1 does the same bowing but is less accented. Extract 2 has a bigger orchestra and a more reverberant acoustic, for example on the final chord, which takes a long time to die away.

Examiner's comments

- Good, detailed points, using specific evidence from the performances. Bar numbers are used to locate convincing detail, such as the accents in bars 531–533.
- A range of aspects are commented upon, showing a detailed understanding of what can be heard in the recordings. The discussion of the solos is perceptive and detailed. There are valid and relevant observations on the orchestral accompaniment. Changes in tempo are described accurately.
- Ideas are well structured, dealing first with the opening, then the tempo changes, finally the end of the passage and the size of the orchestra. There are regular comparisons of both performances. Evidence/bar numbers are consistently used to illustrate the points being made.

8 marks awarded

Prescribed jazz recordings

Make sure that you are studying the correct works for the exam that you will be taking (see page 19).

You are expected to be familiar with the basic factual details about each recording. These include the names of the performers, especially if they have a solo or an important part in the recording. The name of the record company and the date and location of the recordings are also significant. Much of this information can be found on the notes with the CD of the performance.

PERFORMERS, DATES AND LOCATIONS

Alligator Crawl	Ko-Ko	It Ain't Necessarily So
Louis Armstrong and His Hot Seven	Charlie Parker's Reboppers	Miles Davis and the Gil Evans Orchestra
1927	1945	1958
OKeh	Savoy Records	Columbia Records
Chicago	New York	New York
Louis Armstrong, trumpet Johnny Dodds, clarinet Johnny St Cyr, guitar/banjo Lil Hardin-Armstrong, piano John Thomas, trombone Pete Briggs, tuba Baby Dodds, drums	Charlie Parker, alto sax Dizzy Gillespie, trumpet/piano Curly Russell, double bass Max Roach, drums	Miles Davis, trumpet Bill Barber, tuba Paul Chambers, double bass Jimmy Cobb, drums
Based on Alligator Crawl by Fats Waller	Based on Cherokee by Ray Noble	From the album Porgy and Bess Based on the opera by George Gershwin

PERFORMERS, DATES AND LOCATIONS

Hotter Than That	Ko-Ko	Boplicity
Louis Armstrong and His Hot Five	Duke Ellington and His Famous Orchestra	Miles Davis And His Orchestra
1927	1940	1949
OKeh	RCA Victor	Capitol Records
Chicago	Chicago	New York
Louis Armstrong, trumpet/vocals Johnny Dodds, clarinet Lonnie Johnson, guitar Lil Hardin-Armstrong, piano Kid Ory, trombone Johnny St Cyr, banjo	Juan Tizol, valve trombone Joe Nanton, trombone Duke Ellington, piano Jimmy Blanton, double bass Sonny Greer, drums	Gerry Mulligan, baritone sax Miles Davis, trumpet John Lewis, piano Bill Barber, tuba Nelson Boyd, double bass Kenny Clarke, drums
Lil Hardin-Armstrong, original melody Chords based on jazz standard Tiger Rag		Gil Evans, arranger Birth of the Cool, LP format (1957)

DESCRIBING THE MUSIC

Some of the words and phrases used to discuss and describe jazz music are exactly the same as for the prescribed works. Others are very different. Check that you are familiar with these words:

- **Styles**: bebop, big band, New Orleans, straight, swing
- **Forms**: 12-bar blues, 32-bar song form, standards, arrangements, chorus
- **Instrumentation**: brushes, hi-hat, rhythm section, ride cymbal, mutes
- **Techniques and devices**: blue notes, changes, comping, double time, fall-off, glissando, improvisation, riff, scoop, vibrato, walking bass
- **Recording terms**: gramophone, LP, microphone, phonograph, RPM, vinyl.

STRUCTURE

You are expected to be able to: (i) locate the extract in the overall structure of the work, and (ii) be able to describe briefly the music which precedes or follows the extract.

Here is a brief summary of the structure of each of the prescribed jazz recordings. There is no score provided for these, so you have to rely on your aural ability to remember the shape and organisation of each.

JUNE 2011–JANUARY 2013

Louis Armstrong: *Alligator Crawl*

Introduction	2 bars	Trumpet
Chorus 1	12 bars	Clarinet
Chorus 2	12 bars	Ensemble
Link	4 bars	
Solo	25 bars	Trumpet
Chorus 3	12 bars	Guitar
Chorus 4	12 bars	Ensemble

Charlie Parker: *Ko-Ko*

Introduction	32 bars	Alto sax and trumpet
Chorus 1	64 bars	Alto sax solo
Chorus 2	64 bars	
Solo	27 bars	Drums
Coda	28 bars	Alto sax and trumpet

Miles Davis: *It Ain't Necessarily So*

Introduction	9 bars	
Chorus 1	32 bars	AABA
Chorus 2	32 bars	AABA

Chorus 3	32 bars	AABA
Chorus 4	32 bars	AAAA

JUNE 2013–JANUARY 2015

Louis Armstrong: *Hotter Than That*

Introduction	8 bars	Ensemble
Chorus 1	32 bars	Trumpet
Chorus 2	32 bars	Clarinet
Chorus 3	32 bars	Scat singing
Duet	16 bars	Scat singing and guitar
Link	4 bars	Piano
Chorus 4	16 bars	Trombone
	16 bars	Ensemble
Coda	4 bars	Scat singing and Guitar

Duke Ellington: *Ko-Ko*

Introduction	8 bars	
Chorus 1	12 bars	Valve trombone
Chorus 2	12 bars	Trombone
Chorus 3	12 bars	
Chorus 4	12 bars	Piano
Chorus 5	12 bars	3 trumpets
Chorus 6	12 bars	Double bass
Chorus 7	12 bars	Full band
Coda	12 bars	

Miles Davis: *Boplicity*

Chorus 1	32 bars	AABA	Ensemble
Chorus 2	34 bars	AA	Baritone sax
		B: 6 bars	Ensemble
		4 bars	Trumpet
		A	Ensemble
Chorus 3	32 bars + 1 bar	A	Trumpet and ensemble
		A	Trumpet
		B	Piano
		A	Ensemble

DESCRIBING JAZZ: SAMPLE QUESTION

Explain the relationship between the solo and the accompaniment in the extract. (*5 marks*)

There is no score for the jazz recordings. You are expected to take your evidence from the recorded extract.

6 marks	The candidate identifies specific features of both solo and accompaniment, with clear evidence of perceptive listening.
4–5 marks	The candidate identifies a number of features of both solo and accompaniment, with some evidence of perceptive listening.
2–3 marks	The candidate identifies a few features of both solo and accompaniment, with limited evidence of perceptive listening.
1 mark	The candidate identifies perhaps one feature of either solo or accompaniment.
0 marks	No accurate evidence is offered.

SAMPLE ANSWER 1

Charlie Parker: *Ko-Ko*, 1:16–2:07

Parker's solo is fast moving using lots of movement across a wide range. He mixes up long and short phrases, with accents on offbeats, and an unpredictable shape. He uses a quote from *High Society*. The accompaniment is a pizzicato walking bass. Piano has a countermelody and chords. Bass ends in a high register. The B section of the chorus has descending scales and arpeggios. The drums play fast with accents responding to the solo.

Examiner's comments

- There are detailed points about the saxophone solo (fast moving, wide range, varied phrasing and accents, quote from *High Society*, descending scales).
- The features of the accompaniment are described (correct identification of instruments, pizzicato walking bass, piano countermelody and chords, accents in drums).
- Some reference to the relationship between solo and accompaniment ('drums responding to the solo'). Reference to B section shows attempt to locate evidence.

6 marks awarded

SAMPLE ANSWER 2

Miles Davis: *Boplicity*, 0:57–1:25

Baritone sax plays solo at the beginning. Gerry Mulligan plays in the high register. He uses rests between phrases. It is typical of cool jazz style.

Examiner's comments

- A limited number of accurate points about the solo: Baritone sax is correct, also high register, use of silences.
- No comment on the accompaniment.

2 marks awarded

SAMPLE ANSWER 3

> Louis Armstrong: *Hotter Than That*, 0:09–0:45
>
> The trumpet solo is accompanied by the piano, banjo and guitar: comping and strumming chords. He uses syncopation and swing rhythms. Syncopated anacrusis of two notes at the start of each phrase. The phrases of the solo get higher towards the middle of the solo. The rhythm section stops for the highest note. There is a rip up to this note. The solo plays triplet chromatic notes. There are arpeggios in the second half of the chorus.

Examiner's comments

- There is a good level of detail in this answer. Instruments are correctly identified, with some of the techniques used – comping, strumming, rip.
- There is perceptive comment on the melodic features of the solo (syncopation, swung rhythms, reference to anacrusis, ascending overall shape of the melody, chromatic triplets, arpeggios located in the second half).
- Some reference to comping suggests keeping the beat. The answer notices that the accompaniment stops (perception of 'break').
- A detailed answer, showing perceptive listening.

6 marks awarded

SAMPLE ANSWER 4

> Evans/Davis: *It Ain't Necessarily So*, 1:31–1:59
>
> Miles Davis plays the solo. He has scales and arpeggios in a very relaxed style, typical of cool jazz. There is a riff on the horns which is repeated notes. The drums are playing throughout.

Examiner's comments

- The riff in the horns is correctly identified.
- Other comments show a basic level of observation, not really focused on the features of the solo and accompaniment.
- A reference to the walking bass would have improved this answer. Reference to 'drums' lacks detail: for example, the cymbal – is it sticks or brushes?

1 mark awarded

Section C: Essay question

The final question on the paper is an essay on the historical context of the prescribed orchestral works and the jazz recordings. You have to know about the background of these works, and the condition of music and society that existed at the time they were written; the six works are snapshots of their time. As far as this course is concerned, your 'introduction to historical study in music' has begun with these works. You are not expected to learn about other works but to use these works as a starting point for learning about the study of music and its history.

Here are some relevant topics that you could research and revise:

Checklist of contextual topics		
Vivaldi	**Haydn**	**Beethoven**
■ Basso continuo ■ Concertos ■ Development of the early orchestra ■ Early bassoons ■ Employment for musicians in Venice ■ The Pietà and the Ospedali ■ Ritornello form ■ Violin-making.	■ Double wind orchestra ■ Esterházy family ■ *Kapellmeister* at Eszterháza ■ London musical life ■ Natural horns and trumpets ■ The Opera Concert ■ Peter Salomon ■ Publication of the symphonies ■ Subscription concerts.	■ Benefit concerts ■ Brass and woodwind ■ Cadenza ■ Franz Clement ■ Publication and publishers ■ The Romantic movement ■ Tourte bow ■ Vienna ■ Violin technology.

Checklist of contextual topics Prescribed jazz recordings, June 2011–January 2013		
Alligator Crawl	*Charlie Parker's Ko-Ko*	*It Ain't Necessarily So*
■ Louis Armstrong ■ Chicago ■ Hot Five and Hot Seven ■ Improvisation ■ New Orleans style ■ OKeh ■ Rhythm section.	■ Bebop ■ Cherokee ■ Chord extensions ■ Decline of big bands ■ Dizzy Gillespie ■ Drum technique ■ Improvisation ■ Jazz for listening ■ Walking bass.	■ Arranging ■ Claude Thornhill Band ■ Columbia Records ■ Cool jazz ■ Miles Davis' trumpet style ■ Gil Evans ■ LPs ■ *Porgy and Bess* ■ Studio recording.

Checklist of contextual topics Prescribed jazz recordings, June 2013–January 2015		
Hotter Than That	Duke Ellington's *Ko-Ko*	*Boplicity*
■ Louis Armstrong ■ Chicago ■ Lil Hardin-Armstrong ■ Hot Five and Hot Seven ■ Improvisation ■ Lonnie Johnson ■ New Orleans style ■ OKeh ■ Scat singing.	■ Arranging for big band ■ Jimmy Blanton ■ Cotton Club ■ The Ellington effect ■ 'Jungle' style ■ Mutes ■ Radio and recording ■ Swing bands ■ Touring the USA and Europe ■ Walking bass.	■ 78s and LPs ■ Arranging ■ Reaction to bebop ■ *Birth of the Cool* ■ Claude Thornhill Band ■ Miles Davis' trumpet style ■ Gil Evans ■ Miles Davis Nonet.

WHAT EXAMINERS ARE LOOKING FOR

Examiners will mark the essays using the mark grid familiar from longer questions in Sections A and B. Examples of mark schemes can be downloaded from the OCR website. There is also guidance in the OCR specification for A-level Music on the website.

A typical mark grid for essays might contain some key phrases which distinguish each band of marks.

For example, for 16–18 marks (a Grade A) an essay needs to show:

> *Specific knowledge and understanding of the background of the repertoire, supported … by clearly-identified examples of music, mostly well applied towards answering the question. Ideas generally well structured and expressed in language that is good quality with very few lapses in grammar, punctuation and spelling.*

The descriptions for each band of marks show that the examiners are looking at four main aspects of your essays:

■ How well do you know and understand the historical background to the prescribed works?
■ Can you use examples from the prescribed works to support your knowledge?
■ Are you able to answer the question and organise your ideas?
■ Do you express your ideas well and use language accurately?

These four points can be mapped against the marks as shown on the next page.

Grade	Marks	Knowledge of background to the prescribed works	Examples from the music	Relevance and organisation of ideas	Expression and language
A	19–20	Thorough and detailed understanding.	Detailed and specific examples.	Directly answering the question. Ideas are well structured.	Consistently high quality.
	16–18	Specific knowledge and understanding.	Clearly identified examples.	Mostly well applied to answering the question. Generally well structured.	Good quality.
B–E	13–15	Good general knowledge and understanding.	Some accurate references to examples.	Some relevance.	Fairly clearly expressed, in mainly good-quality language.
	10–12	Some knowledge.	A few accurate examples, with little detail.	Not always relevant.	Some weakness in language.
	7–9	Limited knowledge and/or confused understanding.	Not always accurate and/or not well understood.	Not always relevant or accurate.	Poorly expressed, persistent errors in language.
U	4–6	Little knowledge.	Little use of examples.	Little relevance.	Serious weaknesses in language.
	0–3	Very little knowledge.	No examples.	Very few relevant ideas.	Very poor quality.

You may be better at some aspects than others. Your final mark will be a 'best fit'. See the examples below.

SAMPLE ESSAY QUESTIONS

QUESTION 1

Describe the circumstances in which Haydn's 'Drum Roll' Symphony was created.

SAMPLE ANSWER 1

Haydn went to London for two visits. He wrote 12 symphonies, nos. 93–104. The Drum Roll symphony is the penultimate work of the London symphonies. The Drum Roll is featured at the beginning of the symphony to wake the audience up in case they were sleeping. He was invited to London by the violinist Salomon. The horns are used a lot in the symphony to play a horn call. There are two bassoons like Vivaldi but the bassoons do not play the solo.

The violins play the tune, divided into violins 1 and 2. They play dramatic and fast. The brass and timpani is used to make a powerful effect when the tutti is loud. Beethoven uses a bigger orchestra in his violin concerto.

Examiner's comments

- The candidate is aware of the London origin of the symphony, the role of Salomon and the London symphonies. The origin of the nickname is explained. Overall there is a limited amount of historical background given here.
- Examples are not always relevant to the question. There is some awareness of the importance of the horns and the size of the orchestra, but there is little relevant detail.

6 marks awarded

SAMPLE ANSWER 2

Haydn wrote the 'Drum Roll' Symphony for his second visit to London in 1795. It was first performed at the King's Theatre, which had a concert hall at the back of the stage, for an audience of 800 people. This was No. 11 of Haydn's 12 symphonies that are known as the 'London' symphonies.

Haydn was invited to London by Peter Salomon, the London violinist and impresario. Haydn was working for Prince Esterházy as the music director at the court of Eszterháza. When the Prince Nicolaus Esterházy died the new prince did not want so much music at court. Haydn was available to travel to London.

Haydn was already famous when he arrived in London. His music was published and performed all over Europe. In Vienna and Hungary Haydn had been writing for an audience of upper-class nobility. In London there was a large middle-class audience that wanted to pay to attend concerts. Salomon's orchestra had subscription concerts, the Opera Concert. He was in competition with Pleyel, who directed the Professional Concert. Salomon wanted Haydn to visit London to make sure that the Opera Concert won the competition.

Haydn signed a contract with Salomon to write six symphonies for the first visit and six for the second visit in 1795. The contract paid Haydn more money than he earned working for Prince Esterházy, so he was very rich from his visit to London.

The orchestra was very large, much larger than Haydn was used to. It included clarinets, which Haydn had not used before. The players were very good, including some of the players from Pleyel's orchestra, which had been disbanded. Salomon played the violin and led the orchestra but the Drum Roll symphony was led by G.B. Viotti. Haydn played the piano in the orchestra.

Haydn uses effects which the audiences enjoyed, e.g. the drum roll at the start of the symphony, which was very unusual. The last movement starts with a call for the two horns. This is repeated with a melody in the violins which is a folk tune from Croatia. The folk tune made the music very melodic, which was popular with the audience. The audience liked how Haydn used the melody in counterpoint. For example, at the first orchestral tutti Haydn plays the horn tune in the violins and the folk tune is in the bass instruments. This was a very clever effect.

Haydn was very popular in England. He met the King and Queen. Newspapers called Haydn the Shakespeare of music. These are the circumstances in which the 'Drum Roll' Symphony was created.

Examiner's comments

- There is detailed information about the background to the symphony. The candidate is aware of the nature of the audience (middle class, series of subscription concerts, 800 capacity of the King's Theatre) and specific details about performances (Salomon, availability of clarinets, Viotti as leader of the orchestra, Haydn on the piano).
- There are clear and informed comparisons with Eszterháza and Vienna. There is some understanding of the nature of Haydn's contract with Salomon, the difference it would make to him financially, and the competitive nature of professional concerts in London, even if not fully understood.
- Music examples have been used to explain the audience's response to Haydn. There are specific references to the drum roll, use of folk song, use of counterpoint.
- Ideas are relevant, well structured and clearly expressed, using mainly good-quality language.

17 marks awarded

QUESTION 2

How did radio and recording affect the development of music in the twentieth century?

Recording was very important in the 1920s. When Louis Armstrong was performing with his band recording was difficult. The players had to stand around one microphone. Loud instruments like drums had to be at the back so the needle would not jump. The music was recorded on wax discs and then made into shellac. The recording limit was 3 minutes so songs had to be cut down to fit the discs. The room had to be hot because of the wax so the band could not play for long.

When Miles Davis and his band recorded conditions were very different. A studio was used so the recording was better. There was microphones for all the instruments and the engineer could balance the sound of all the instruments.

> Radio was also very important. There were many radio stations all over America playing jazz music. If a band was on the radio more people would come to hear them live.

Examiner's comments

- Some information on recording methods in the 1920s is included, but there is very little on the development of the music. The only relevant comment is on the 3-minute restriction on Armstrong. There is some understanding of improvements in technology for Miles Davis, but again this is not related to the music.
- There is a basic understanding of the existence of radio stations in America and the opportunities they provided to make bands more popular and commercially successful. There is no detail or supporting evidence.
- Overall there is little relevant information here.

4 marks awarded

Check that you are answering the question. The answer here suggests that the student believes the question is about recording and recording technology. In fact the question wants to know about the effect of recording on music. Detail on 1920s recording technology is relevant, but it needs to be followed up with an explanation of how the music, musicians and audiences were affected.

A higher mark would be achieved if some of these points were included:

Background to the repertoire	Possible evidence that can be used	
	June 2011–January 2013	June 2013–January 2015
1920s; early jazz recordings; limits of technology; 78rpm; 3-minute limit.	*Alligator Crawl*: alternating solos and ensemble passages; tuba used for bass.	*Hotter Than That*: short sections of solos and ensemble sections; unexpected guitar chords to finish piece.
Role of recording companies in promoting jazz; rise of 'star' soloists.	OKeh company; recordings of Hot Five/Hot Seven; promoting Louis Armstrong; longer solos.	OKeh company; recordings of Hot Five; promoting Louis Armstrong; longer solos; use of scat singing.
Radio and recording contracts; commercial opportunities.	Charlie Parker: contract with Savoy; fame of recordings; model for younger artists, e.g. Miles Davis.	Duke Ellington: radio broadcasts from Cotton Club establish early fame; recordings led to European tours.
1950s; development of the LP; longer recordings; albums; studio technology.	*It Ain't Necessarily So*: extended album based on *Porgy and Bess*; sound balance can include alto flutes; intended for home listening not live performance.	*Boplicity*: unsuccessful at first; later released as part of *Birth of Cool* album.

You do not have to refer to any works which are not the prescribed works. You can achieve the highest marks without mentioning other works. You will get credit for using your knowledge if it is relevant.

If you are writing about the jazz works, explaining the background to the recordings is your main priority. Referring to examples is important in order to access the higher grades. Look at the following example for the second point on the table above.

EXAMPLE OF DETAILED PARAGRAPHS: ROLE OF RECORDING COMPANIES IN PROMOTING JAZZ, RISE OF 'STAR' SOLOISTS.

The 1920s saw the growth of a number of record companies, which had a strong influence on the development of jazz. When he moved to Chicago, Louis Armstrong made a series of recordings for the OKeh Phonograph Company, playing with a band known as the Hot Five. Later the number was expanded to the Hot Seven. The band did not play live but were specially recruited for the recordings. The recordings were popular and successful. As part of the promotion of the discs, OKeh issued a free photograph of Louis Armstrong with some of the recordings. He became famous even to people who could not hear his live performances in New York or Chicago.

His recordings also made him a model for young trumpeters, who copied his solos from the recordings, imitating his style of playing rips and falls, and his rhythmic swing. His playing is bold and dramatic, building up to the highest notes in a very exciting way. The solos were published in books so that trumpeters could learn them. OKeh soon realised that Armstrong was commercially more important than the rest of the band. The long solos in *Alligator Crawl* and *Hotter Than That* are there so that listeners can admire his playing. The New Orleans collective improvisation sections and the solos for other players (for example Johnny Dodds on the clarinet) became less important than listening to Armstrong, the star soloist. The New Orleans style became less popular because audiences wanted to hear soloists.

Examiner's comments

- Detailed contextual information on OKeh, the origins of the Hot Five and Seven. There is a good understanding of the commercial importance of Louis Armstrong, his influence on other soloists and how the demand for soloists was linked to the decline of the New Orleans style.
- There is specific evidence from the prescribed recordings, including the reference to techniques used by Armstrong in his solos and the importance of long solos compared to other sections.
- Well written, with ideas linked together to make clear paragraphs. If the essay were to continue with this level of knowledge and evidence, it would be on course to get full marks.

Glossary

Acciaccatura. A very short ornamental note played just before a principal melodic note.

Anacrusis. The note or notes that form an upbeat (or upbeats) to the first downbeat of a phrase.

Antiphony. A technique where two instrumental groups or two choirs alternate in dialogue.

Appoggiatura. An ornamental note that falls on the beat as a dissonance and then resolves by step onto the main note.

Arpeggio. A chord in which the notes are played one after the other rather than at the same time.

Articulation. The manner in which a series of notes are played with regard to their separation or connection – for example, staccato (separated) or legato (connected).

Atonal. Western music that is not in a key or a mode. Often dissonant.

Augmentation. The lengthening of rhythmic values of a previously heard melody (for example in a fugue), or the widening of an interval.

Auxiliary note. A non-harmony note which is a step above (upper auxiliary) or below (lower auxiliary) the harmony note and returns to it.

Binary form. Two-part structure (AB), usually with both sections repeated.

Broken chord. A chord in which the notes are played one after the other rather than at the same time.

Call-and-response. A pair of phrases, performed by different musicians, in which the second phrase is heard as a reply to the first. This term normally refers to jazz, pop and world music.

Chord extension. Chords which add additional 3rds to the third and fifth degree of a triad, creating a 7th, 9th, 11th or 13th.

Chromatic. The use of non-diatonic notes (notes which are not in the current key).

Circle of 5ths. A series of chords whose roots are each a 5th lower (or a 4th higher) than the previous one. For example, Em–Am–Dm–G–C.

Compound metre. Time signature in which the beat divides into three: $\frac{6}{8}$, $\frac{9}{8}$, $\frac{12}{8}$.

Consonant. Intervals or chords which are stable and sound pleasant (for example, unisons, 3rds, 6ths), as opposed to its opposite, dissonant.

Continuo. Short for 'basso continuo', the continuo instruments form the accompaniment in Baroque music. It may include instruments such as the harpsichord (capable of playing full harmony) and a cello or bassoon reinforcing the bass line.

Contrapuntal. see **Counterpoint**.

Contrary motion. Movement of two parts in opposite directions to each other.

Countermelody. An independent melody which complements a more prominent theme.

Counterpoint. A texture in which two or more melodic lines, each one significant in itself, are played together at the same time. When describing this kind of texture, you would use the adjective **contrapuntal**.

Diatonic. Using notes that belong to the current key.

Diminished 7th. A four-note chord made up of a diminished triad plus a diminished 7th above the root.

Diminution. A compositional technique in which the durations of the notes of a motif or phrase are proportionally reduced in a restatement of it.

Dominant 7th. A four-note chord built on the dominant (5th) note of the scale. It includes the dominant triad plus a minor 7th above the root.

Dominant pedal. A pedal on the fifth degree of the scale of the prevailing key.

Dotted rhythm. A rhythm that contains pairs of notes in the pattern 'long-short'. The first note is dotted and the second is a third of the dotted note's value (e.g. dotted crotchet–quaver).

Double-stopping. A string technique of playing more than one string at a time.

Glissando. A slide between two notes.

Grace note. A quick ornamental note that comes before a main note.

Ground bass. Repeating bass, usually four or eight bars in length, with changing music in the other parts. Popular in Baroque music.

Harmonic. Sometimes known as flageolet note, a technique of lightly touching the string (e.g. on a violin) to produce a high, flute-like sound.

Harmonic rhythm. The rate at which harmony changes in a piece.

Homophonic. A texture in which one part has a melody and the other parts accompany. In contrast to a polyphonic texture, in which each part has independent melodic interest.

Imitative. A contrapuntal device in which a distinct melodic idea in one part is immediately copied by another part, often at a different pitch, while the first part continues with the other music. The imitation is not always strict, but the basic rhythmic and melodic outline should be heard.

Imperfect cadence. The end of a phrase harmonised with two chords, the second of which is a dominant chord.

Interrupted cadence. At the end of a phrase, a dominant chord followed by almost any chord other than the tonic chord. The second of these two chords interrupts the expected resolution of the dominant chord to the tonic.

Interval. The distance between two notes. For example, the interval between the notes F and A is a 3rd (A is the third note of the F major scale).

Key signature. A group of flats or sharps placed immediately after the clef at the beginning of a stave or immediately after a double bar. These flats and sharp signs indicate which notes are to be played flat or sharp whenever they appear on the same stave (unless they are contradicted by accidentals).

Legato. A smooth articulation of music without any breaks between successive notes.

Leger line. Additional lines used above or beneath the stave to represent notes that fall outside of its range.

Major and minor. Describe different types of intervals, chords, keys and scales. Minor intervals are smaller than major intervals by a semitone (e.g. F to A is a major 3rd, whereas F to A♭ is a minor 3rd). A major chord, key or scale contains a major above the tonic, whereas a minor chord, scale or key contains a minor 3rd (e.g. a D major chord contains the notes D–F♯–A, while a D minor chord uses the notes D–F♮–A).

Marcato. Accented notes, played with emphasis.

Mode. Seven-note scales that can be created using only the white notes of a piano keyboard. The dorian can be played beginning on D (i.e. D–E–F–G–A–B–C–D), the mixolydian on G, the aeolian on A and the ionian on C. These interval patterns can then be transposed to any other note. For example, dorian beginning on G (or G dorian) would be G–A–B–C–D–E–F–G.

Modulation. The process of changing key.

Monophonic. A musical texture that uses a single melodic line.

Mordent. A melodic ornament of two types: a) the lower mordent, which consists of the written note, the note a step below it and the written note again, and b) the upper mordent, which consists of the written note, the note a step above it and the written note again.

Octave. An interval formed from two notes that are 12 semitones apart. Both notes have the same name.

Ornament. Small musical additions that decorate a melody.

Ostinato. A repeating melodic, harmonic or rhythmic motif, heard continuously throughout part or the whole of a piece.

Passing note. A non-essential note filling the gap between two consonant notes a 3rd apart.

Pedal note. A sustained or continuously repeated pitch, often in the bass, that is heard against changing harmonies. A pedal on the fifth degree of the scale (known as the dominant pedal) tends to generate excitement, while a pedal on the key note (known as the tonic pedal) tends to create a feeling of repose.

Perfect cadence. A dominant chord followed by a tonic chord at the end of a phrase.

Phrasing. In performance the execution of longer groups of notes which follow natural patterns of the music. 'Articulation' may be used to refer to phrasing over a shorter group of notes. Phrases may be indicated by the composer but the skill and judgement of the performer is also important in creating a successful performance.

Pitch. The depth or height of a note. Pitch can be measured in absolute terms by counting the number of vibrations per second of the source of the sound.

Pizzicato. A direction to pluck notes on a string instrument.

Plagal cadence. A subdominant chord followed by a tonic chord at the end of a phrase.

Polyphonic. A texture consisting of two or more equally important melodic lines heard together. In contrast to a homophonic texture, in which one part has the melody and the other parts accompany. The term polyphonic has a similar meaning to contrapuntal, but is more often used for vocal rather than instrumental music.

Portamento. A slide between two notes.

Relative minor/major. Keys that have the same key signature but a different tonic. The tonic of a relative minor is three semitones below the tonic of its relative major (e.g. C major and A minor).

Riff. A short, catchy melodic or rhythmic idea that is repeated throughout a jazz or pop song.

Ritornello. A Baroque device where the repeated tutti section is used as a refrain; most often in the first or last movement of a concerto, or in arias or choral works.

Ritornello form. Standard form of first and last movements of the Baroque concerto, alternating tutti ritornelli with solo or ripieno (small group) sections.

Rubato. The alteration of rhythm, particularly in a melodic line, by lengthening and shortening notes but keeping an overall consistent tempo.

Scale. A sequence of notes that move by step either upwards or downwards. Different types of scales have different patterns of intervals.

Scotch snap. A two-note dotted rhythm which has the shorter note on the beat. Usually an on-beat semiquaver followed by an off-beat dotted quaver. Also known as lombardic rhythm.

Sequence. Immediate repetition of a melodic or harmonic idea at a different pitch, or a succession of different pitches.

Sforzando. Strongly accented.

Simple time. A metre in which the main beat is sub-divided into two equal portions (e.g. a crotchet beat divided into two quavers). Opposite of compound time.

Sonata form. Typical first movement form of the Classical and Romantic periods. In three sections – exposition, development, recapitulation – often based on two groups of melodic material in two contrasting keys (first subject, second subject).

Staccato. Detached. Refers to notes that are held for less time than their value indicates, so they are shortened and separated from each other.

Subdominant. The fourth degree of a diatonic scale.

Syncopation. Placing the accents in parts of the bar that are not normally emphasised, such as on weak beats or between beats, rather than in the expected place on strong beats.

Tempo. The speed of the music.

Ternary form. A musical structure of three sections. The outer sections are similar and the central one contrasting (ABA).

Texture. The relationship between the various simultaneous lines in a passage of music, dependant on such features as the number and function of the parts and the spacing between them.

Tonic pedal. A pedal on the first degree of the scale of the prevailing key.

Tremolo. A musical effect that refers to a very quick and continuous repetition of a single note (on bowed or plucked string instruments) or of two alternating notes (on keyboard instruments).

Trill. An ornament consisting of a rapid alternation of two adjacent pitches.

Triplet. A group of three equal notes played in the time normally taken by two of the same type.

Turn. A four-note ornament comprising the note a step above the written note, the written note, the note a step below the written note and the written note again.